Carving Hummingbirds

by

Charles Solomon

and

David Hamilton

1970 Broad Street
East Petersburg, PA 17520

Except where otherwise noted, drawings are by Dale Crawford and photography by Dave Hamilton.

Grateful acknowledgment is hereby given to the following for permission to reprint materials or reproduce photographs:

Male structural characteristics and *Stages in wing action during hovering flight* © Paul Johnsgard.
Photograph of hovering male ruby-throated hummingbird © Luke Wade.
Photograph of hovering broad-tailed hummingbird © Phil Dotson.
Photograph of perched broad-tailed hummingbird © Dave and Steve Maslowski.
Reference photographs pages ii, iii, iv, Arnette Heidcamp

Publisher: Alan Giagnocavo
Project Editor: Ayleen Stellhorn
Desktop Specialist: Robert Altland, Altland Design
Cover Photography: Bob Polett
ISBN#1–56523–064–7

To order your copy of this book,
please send check or money order
for cover price plus $2.50 to:
Fox Chapel Book Orders
1970 Broad Street
East Petersburg, PA 17520

Try your favorite book supplier first!

Second Printing

Printed in China

Dedication

We dedicate this book to our families,
who have been very supportive of our work.

Chuck Solomon is a professional biologist and an affiliate faculty member in the Fishery and Wildlife Biology Department at Colorado State University. He has been teaching carving classes and participating in carving competitions for over 10 years. He has won more than 80 ribbons at shows in Colorado, Alaska, and Canada, including a Best of Show and several Best of Division. Chuck has also judged the Colorado Open and Pikes Peak Whittlers carving shows. His work consists primarily of songbirds and waterfowl, both realistic and interpretative.

Chuck currently lives in the Sacramento, California area, where he carves and teaches classes. For more information, contact Chuck at (916) 683-4996. You may also write to him: c/o Fox Chapel Publishing, 1970 Broad Street, East Petersburg, PA 17520.

Dave Hamilton is an ecologist by profession, working primarily in the area of wetland management. He has been carving and competing in shows for about eight years. While Dave enjoys carving a variety of bird species, he specializes in the wading birds common to the wetlands he works on professionally, and hummingbirds. Dave has competed in a number of woodcarving competitions and has won first place, Best in Division, and Best in Show ribbons for his carvings of hovering hummingbirds of various species.

Dave lives in Fort Collins, Colorado, where he carves and teaches classes. Dave can be reached at (970) 482–8308. You may also write to him: c/o Fox Chapel Publishing, 1970 Broad Street, East Petersburg, PA 17520.

Acknowledgments

This book would not have been possible without the help and encouragement of a number of people. First, we would like to thank Pam Johnson at Mountain Woodcarvers in Estes Park, Colorado, who suggested the idea for this book and put us in contact with Fox Chapel. Special thanks go to Alan Giagnocavo at Fox Chapel, who was continually enthusiastic about our project and who helped us through the publishing process, and to Ayleen Stellhorn, our project editor. Our sincerest thanks go to our friend, Dale Crawford, who did the excellent drawings found throughout the book, and to Paul Vohs, who reviewed some of the early drafts. Also, we thank Luke Wade, Phil Dotson, and Steve and Dave Maslowski for providing the gorgeous photographs of hummingbirds, and Paul Johnsgard for providing the figures comparing hummingbird species and showing hummingbird wing movements in Chapter 1. This second printing also features some stunning photography by Arnette Heidcamp, best-selling author of *A Hummingbird in My House*.

We would also like to thank the many carvers that we have learned from over the years. We would like to specifically acknowledge Bob Guge, Phil Galatas, Rosalyn Daisey, Scott Yablonski, and Dick Pillmore; their classes and books have provided many of the techniques and approaches that we have combined and melded into our own carving and painting styles.

Finally, and most importantly, we would like to thank our families (Mary Ann Solomon and Tina, Becky, and Meghan Hamilton) for their understanding and support throughout this longer-than-expected project, and our parents for their encouragement throughout our lives.

Introduction

Bird carvings are vignettes of nature. The extent to which they succeed is a function of craftsmanship, accuracy, capturing the essences of the species, and artistry of design. These are also the four judging criteria established by the Ward Foundation for the World Championship Wildfowl Carving Competition. The Foundation describes these criteria as follows. Craftsmanship refers to technical skills; how well the bird and habitat are carved and painted. Accuracy involves the scientific correctness of the bird and the habitat. For example, does the bird have the correct number of tail feathers, and are they the correct shape? Essence of the species is a more abstract concept; does the carving capture an attitude in wood? If your carving was seen only in silhouette, would the body position, the cock of the head, and the activity in which the subject was engaged capture the essence of the species such that a viewer could identify the bird without seeing any feather details or colors? Finally, artistry involves overall design and composition; the way in which line, form, content, color, and mass interact.

In this book we focus primarily on the first two criteria. The projects we describe contain step-by-step instructions for accurately carving and painting a broad-tailed hummingbird perched on a branch and a ruby-throated hummingbird hovering and feeding from a red morning-glory. The introductory chapter on hummingbirds and the patterns for these projects provide accurate reference material for these projects. We hope that the patterns we have provided and the associated bases also capture some of the essence of these birds and provide a pleasing composition. Capturing the essence of hummingbirds requires that you study hummingbirds in their natural environment, which cannot be passed on in a book. We do, however, provide references for books that describe the life and behavior of hummingbirds in more detail. We have briefly mentioned a few design and composition concepts applied in these projects, but leave a more detailed treatment of these ideas to various art books and a few magazine articles we have cited in the text.

Finally, a few general notes concerning the book. The projects are presented in order of difficulty. The perched broad-tailed hummingbird in Chapter 3 is on an intermediate level, and the hovering ruby-throated hummingbird feeding from a red morning-glory in Chapters 4 and 5 is the most extensive project. Throughout the text, we mention specific tools that we use. Many tools can be used to accomplish the same task, and we are merely pointing out the tools that work best for us. You should feel free to experiment and use whatever works best for you. Lastly, we have purposely mixed units of measurement, using millimeters for measurement of the birds (which is what we generally work in) and inches for things like drill bit sizes, wood thicknesses, and copper tubing diameters (which is how these items are usually labeled). Hopefully this will not cause any confusion. Most importantly, we hope you learn a few new things from this book and that you enjoy the projects we have presented.

Table of Contents

Assortment of hummingbirds that can be used for reference. Please note that not all of the birds in the photos are depicted in the two hummingbird carvings in the book. Plumage of the female Rufous hummingbird can vary greatly.

Top – *Back view of feeding bird. Note highlights on back. Female Rufous. Delphinium flower shown.*

Middle – *Note variation of wing position. Female Rufous. Western Columbine shown (Aquilegia Formoser).*

Bottom – *This bird appears to be backing from the flower. Note dramatic wing twist. Female Rufous. Passiflora Vitifolia shown.*

Top – *Top view of head. Note contour where wings meet the body. Female Rufous. Passiflora Citrina shown.*

Middle – *Front view of bird. Note breast detail. Female Rufous. Snapdragon flowers shown.*

Bottom – *Note darker value where wing feathers overlap. Female Rufous. Manzanita flowers shown (Arctostaphylos Spales).*

Top – *Stretching its neck while feeding. Female Rufous. Calliandra shown.*

Middle – *Note transition between belly and lower tail coverts. Female Rufous. Pentas flowers shown.*

Bottom – *Young hummingbird. Female Rufous. Notice how short the bill and tail is on a nestling hummingbird.*

Chapter One
Hummingbirds

To Audubon, the hummingbird was a "glittering fragment of rainbow... with motions so graceful as they are light and airy, pursuing its course and yielding new delights wherever it is seen."

Hummingbirds are native to and occur only in the Western Hemisphere. They are found in North, Central, and South America, and the islands of the Caribbean. Although they are highly adaptable, hummingbirds aren't found in the Eastern Hemisphere; the ocean barrier appears too difficult to cross during migration.

The hummingbird family *(Trochilidae)* includes 338 species and 116 genera. The center of abundance and diversity for hummingbirds is the equatorial belt across South America where more than 50 percent are found. Ecuador supports the largest number of hummingbird species (163) followed by Columbia (135), Peru (100), Venzuella (90), and Brazil (90). There is a progressive decline in species north of Panama.

Only 13 species breed in the United States, but 16-19 species have been observed in the U.S. Only one species, the ruby-throated hummingbird, lives east of the Mississippi River (Figure 1:1). One of the more abundant species in the Rocky Mountains area is the broad-tailed hummingbird (Figures 1:2 and 1:3). Structural characteristics of 15 male hummingbirds found within the United States are provided in Figure 1:4.

Hummingbirds range in size from the bee hummingbird of Cuba, the smallest bird in the world (about $2^{1}/_{4}$ inches long) to the *Patagona gigas* of the Andes, which is about $8^{1}/_{2}$ inches long.

Human interaction with and interest in hummingbirds is probably due to their size, exquisite plumage, and superb flight.

Figure 1:1 *Ruby-throated hummingbird (copyright by Luke Wade).*

IRIDESCENCE

Names such as red-tailed comet, Andean hill-star, blue-tufted starthroat, glittering-brilliant emerald, gilded sapphire, green-backed fire-crown, and amethyst woodstar were used by naturalists T. Narosky and D. Yzarieta in *Guia Para La Identificacion De Las Aves De Argentina Y Urugay* to describe various hummingbirds. Seen from a specific angle, the head and gorget of most hummingbirds appear to glow with metallic brilliance referred to as iridescence.

Colors in most birds are generally produced by pigments. The pigments absorb specific wavelengths of light and reflect other wavelengths in random directions. The color or hue of a pigmented body changes little with various angles of vision. However, color may also be produced by the physical structure of colorless bodies. Color may be caused by differential scattering of light, refraction, or a combination of the two. On the ruby-throated and broad-tailed hummingbirds covered in this book, the red gorget feather and the green body feather colors are produced by such physical structures.

Thanks to the pioneering work of amateur ornithologist Crawford Greenwalt, we now understand the mechanism of iridescence in hummingbirds. The barbule of the upper one third of the iridescent feathers contains small elliptical granules, called platelets. These platelets, which vary in size, are filled with air bubbles. The thickness of platelets and the quantity of air inside determines the color. Some feathers reflect light in only one direction whereas others reflect light in all directions. (See Tyrrell (1984) or Johnsgard (1983) for a more complete description of iridescence.)

FLIGHT

The flight of hummingbirds is as intriguing as their brilliantly colored plumage. They fly by rotating the entire wing with minimal or no wrist or elbow flexing. This unique method of flight allows forward, backward, sideways, upside down, and hovering movement. In order to accomplish these remarkable aerial gymnastics, the hummingbird wing muscles are quite large. They account for 25-30 percent of the entire weight of the hummingbird, more than any other bird. The smallest hummingbirds have

Figure 1:2 *Broad-tailed hummingbird (copyright by Phil Dotson).*

Figure 1:3 *Broad-tailed hummingbird (copyright by Dave and Steve Maslowski).*

the most rapid wingbeat of all birds, possibly 200 beats per second during courtship displays. An average hummingbird wingbeat is 50-60 beats per second in forward flight.

There is a close relationship between wing length and the rate of wing beat, which is also true in other flying birds. Figure 1:5 shows the wing action during hovering flight. Wing position during flight other than hovering would be somewhat different.

A hummingbird has the ability to achieve practically full speed as soon as it takes wing. This is potentially quite useful in avoiding predators. It can also approach its perch at full speed and stop abruptly, a characteristic that could be disastrous for large birds or commercial aircraft.

FEEDING

The metabolic rate of hummingbirds is extremely high, the highest of any warm blooded animal. It has been estimated that humans would have to consume double their weight in food per day if their metabolic rates were the same as a hummingbird. To maintain this high metabolic rate, the hummingbird must consume large quantities of food. Approximately 50 percent of its weight in sugar is eaten daily. (See Tyrrell (1984) for greater detail on feeding and metabolism.)

Hummingbirds feed primarily on flowers and turn nectar into food energy. Based on a study of sugar content in preferred flowers in the United States and the tropics, the average sugar content was 25 percent. Flowers containing less than 25 percent sugar were avoided. Hummingbirds collect nectar by a licking motion with their tongue, which is about as long as their bill and can be greatly extended. Thus, the hummingbird's bill does not have to be completely inside a flower in order to gather nectar. They also eat insects and spiders to obtain necessary protein and vitamins. Frequently they will catch insects in the air similar to flycatchers. They appear to consume more insects during rainy periods and when nectar is scarce or unavailable.

Food habits of hummingbirds feeding on flowers make them attractive subjects for carvers. The types, colors, and diversity of habitats is almost limitless. If you have a flower garden, you have access to not only watch hummingbirds, but live models from which to sculpt habitat.

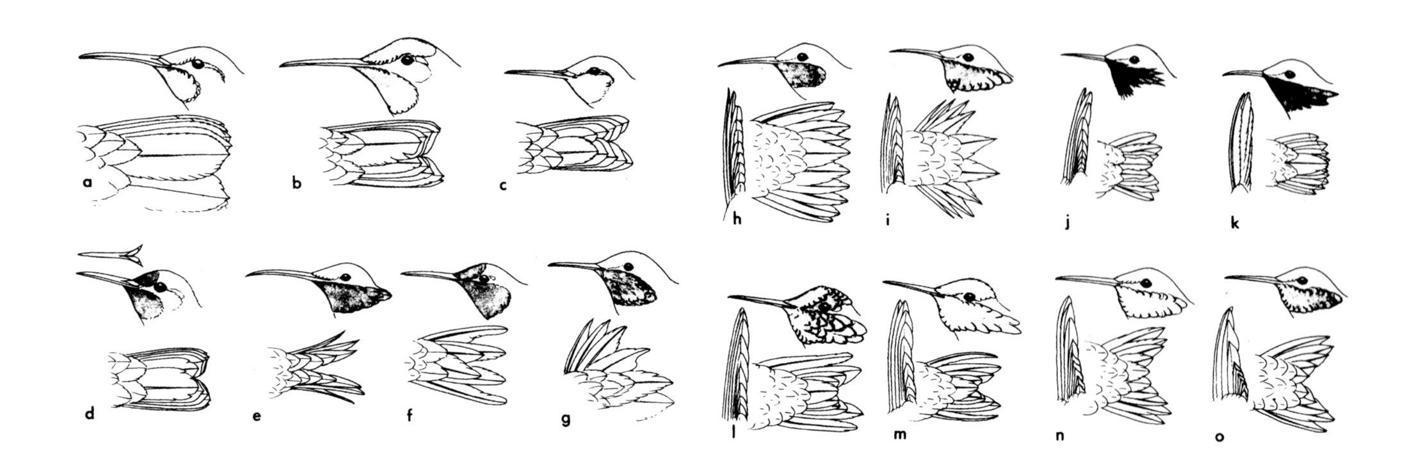

Figure 1:4 *Male structural characteristics of (a) blue-throated hummingbird, (b) Rivoli hummingbird, (c) broad-billed hummingbird, (d) white-eared hummingbird, (e) lucifer hummingbird, (f) Bahama woodstar, (g) rufous hummingbird, (h) broad-tailed hummingbird, (i) Allen hummingbird, (j) calliope hummingbird, (k) bumblebee hummingbird, (l) Anna hummingbird, (m) Costa hummingbird, (n) black-chinned hummingbird, and (o) ruby-throated hummingbird (from Johnsgard 1983)*

Figure 1:5 *Stages in wing action during hovering flight in a hummingbird, in side and dorsal views. Numbered points on the central diagram indicate location of wingtip at successive stages. (from Johnsgard 1983).*

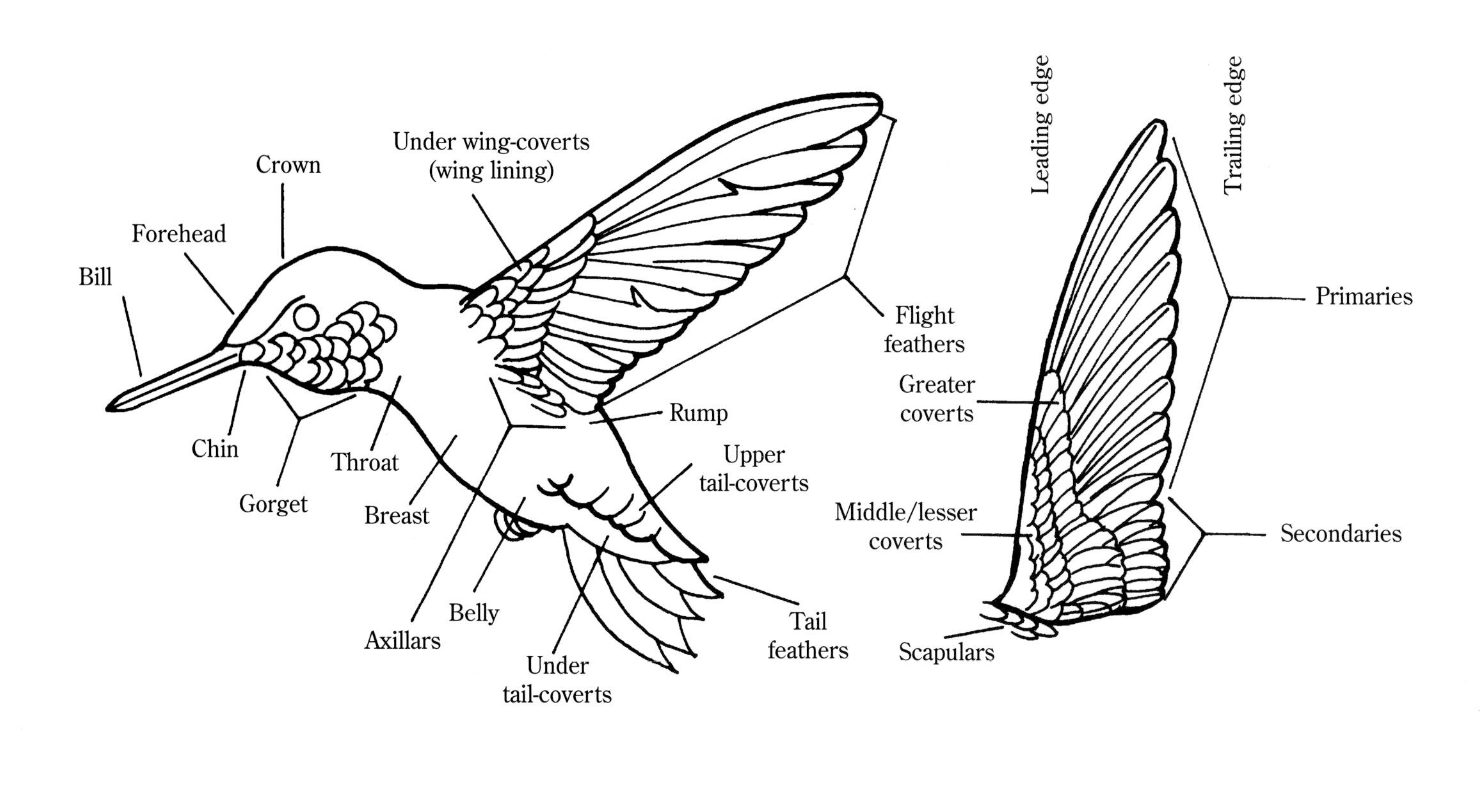

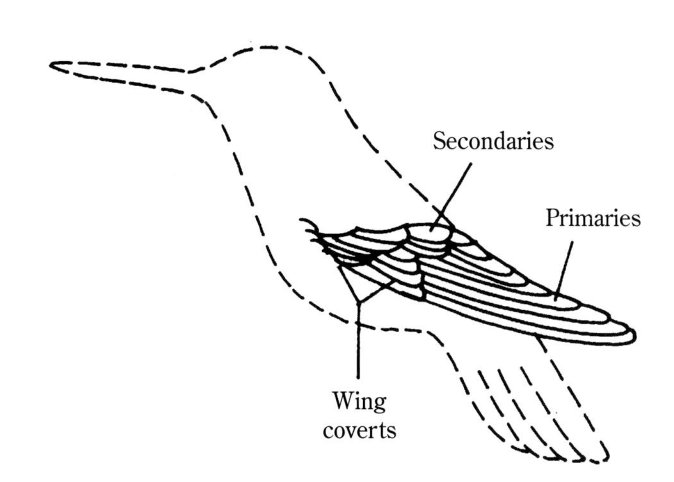

Figure 1:6 *Hummingbird topography. Throughout this book, we will be referring to various parts and feather groups of a hummingbird. The anatomy diagram in Figure 1:6 is provided as a reference for the terminology we will be using.*

Chapter Two

Tools and Supplies

There is no shortage of tools available for carvers. It is not our intention to discuss the wide variety of carving tools and supplies, rather we will discuss primarily those used in completing the projects in this book.

Basically, all you really need for these projects is a sharp knife, sandpaper, a burning pen, paints, and a paint brush. However, we use power tools and several types of grinders and rotary cutters to assist in completing many of the tasks described herein.

WOODS

Basswood and tupelo are the two most popular woods used for carving birds; basswood being the most common. Basswood has a tight grain, carves and burns well, and is readily available at most carving supply stores. Tupelo grinds and burns well. The surface of tupelo is relatively smooth after use of power tools, which is an advantage over many other woods, including basswood. Sugar pine and jelutong are quite popular in some areas of the country. Any of these woods can be used for the hummingbird projects in this book. We used basswood for the perched hummingbird and tupelo for the hovering hummingbird.

KNIVES

There are many shapes and sizes of knives available through woodcarving shops and specialty stores (Figure 2:1). The most commonly used knives for carving birds are probably those produced by the Warren Tool Company and Cheston Knotts. The Lyons and Taylor knives are popular in our area.

It is important to have a knife with a high quality steel blade that will hold an edge and can be sharpened without too much difficulty. The knives mentioned above possess these desirable qualities.

Having more than one shape and length of blade may be important for many projects. For

Figure 2:1 *Knives from left to right: 1st two C. Knotts, next 2 Lyons, G. Taylor, and last 2 Warren.*

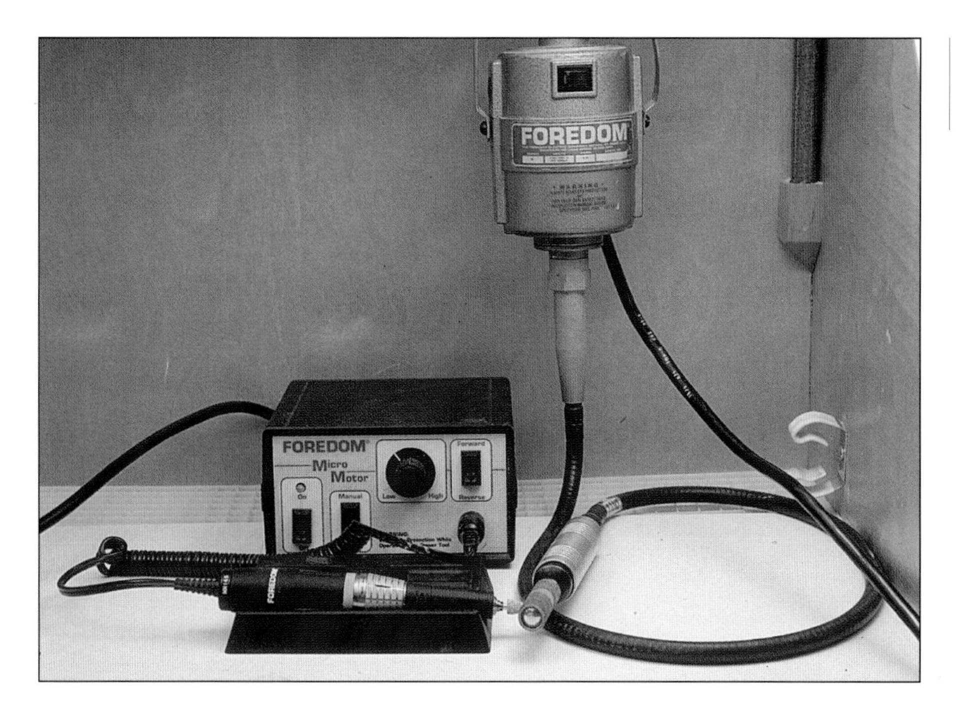

Figure 2:2 *Foredom 1/8 hp flexible shaft and high speed grinder.*

example, a knife with a three-inch blade would not be the best choice for a hummingbird, yet it may be highly desirable for a half- or full-sized decoy. The way the handle fits in your hand is important since you may be holding it for long periods of time. Test the fit of the handle in your hand if possible before purchasing a knife.

POWER TOOLS

Many carvers today, ourselves included, use power tools to assist in carving. The use of power tools and the various cutting tools available can be extremely effective in accomplishing specific carving tasks, such as undercutting wings, making "lumps and bumps," or obtaining soft feather detail. Now that carving is becoming more popular, a number of companies are making power grinders and micro motor tools for carvers. We will be using the Foredom flexible shaft and micro motor high-speed grinder for projects in this book (Figure 2:2).

A flexible shaft tool with the capability to hold larger tungsten carbide bits and sanding drums is useful in removing large amounts of wood quickly. The Foredom Company manufactures several handpieces for their flexible shaft tool. The high speed grinders (20,000 to 45,000 rpm) are most useful in creating lumps and bumps and creating fine feather detail. There are a number of steel, tungsten carbide, ruby, and diamond bits available for the power tools (Figures 2:3 and 2:4). Make sure the bit you are using is rated for the rpm of the motor tool.

Additionally, it is extremely important for you to use safety glasses or goggles and a dust mask or vacuum box when using power equipment. A report from the National Institution for Occupational Safety and Health stated that breathing wood dust can cause a number of respiratory problems including emphysema and lung cancer. The bacteria, fungi, or volatile oils in some woods can also cause breathing problems. OSHA (Office of Safety and Health Administration, Department of Labor) guidelines indicate that exposure to wood dust in excess of 5 mg per cubic meter of air is hazardous to your health. To put that in more understandable terms, that limit would be reached in my shop (15 feet by 15 feet with 8-foot ceilings) when there are only eight thousandths (.008) of an ounce of wood dust in the air! Dust collection systems come in all sizes and price ranges. Some are large with built in

Figure 2:3 *Various tungsten carbide bits and cushioned drum sanders.*

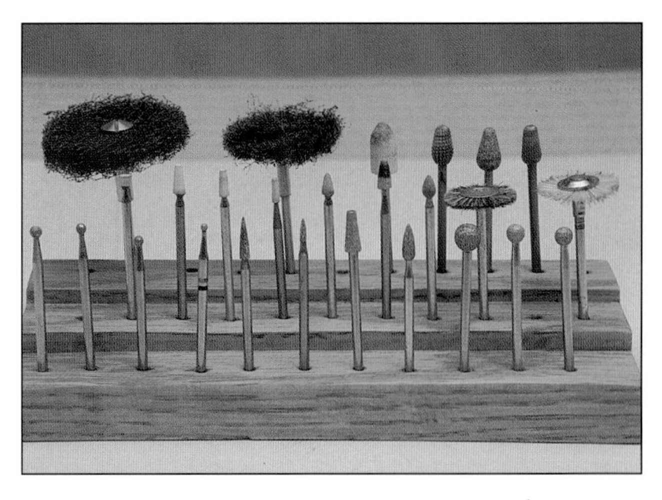

Figure 2:4 *Assortment of ruby carvers, diamond bits, stones, defuzzing pads, and rotary brushes.*

work benches (e.g. the one in the back of Figure 2:5), some are portable (e.g. the one down in front of Figure 2:5), some sit in your lap as you carve, and others attach directly to your power carving tools. Carving magazines have even had plans for making dust boxes out of cardboard boxes, window fans, and furnace filters. Dust masks can help but the dust particles are still suspended in the air and can be breathed into your lungs after you are done carving (not to mention the mess the dust can make when it finally settles in your shop or the rest of your house). The bottom line is that if you are going to power carve, you should wear safety glasses and have some type of dust collection system. Protecting your eyes and lungs is a good investment and will help you enjoy carving long into the future. They should be among the most important and useful tools in your workshop.

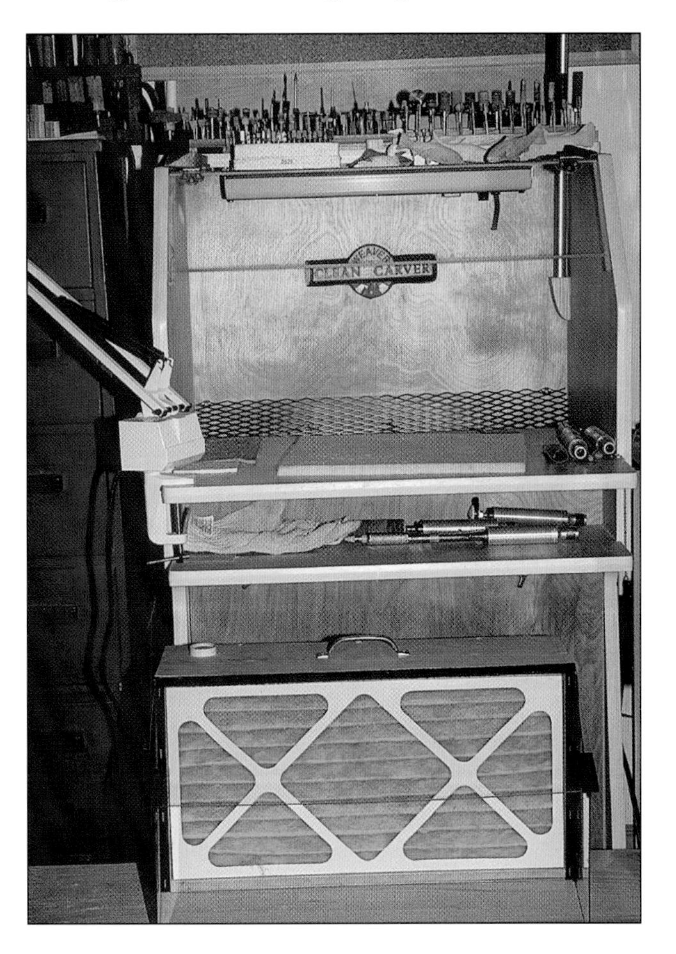

Figure 2:5 *Desk model and portable dust boxes.*

BURNING TOOLS

Several companies manufacture burning tools (Figure 2:6). It is important to have a rheostat to control the heat. Some of the more expensive burners include a potentiometer, which provides a constant heat output. It is desirable to have a burning unit that accepts interchangeable hand pieces. Different species of wood require different temperatures to achieve the same effects, and special effects can be created by modifying the heat of the burning tip. For the projects described in this book, we used several burning pens (Figure 2:7). They will be described in detail later.

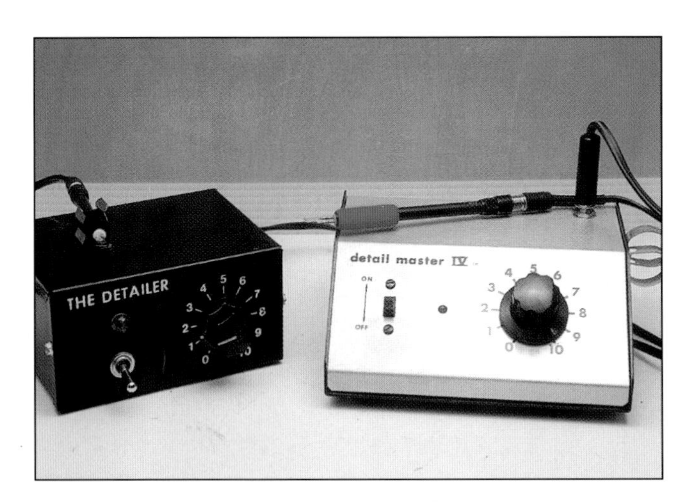

Figure 2:6 *Colwood Detailer and Detail Master burning systems.*

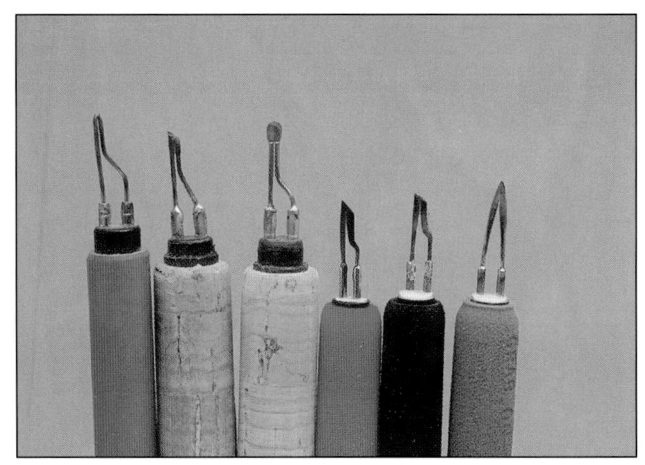

Figure 2:7 *Various shapes and sizes of burning pens.*

PAINTS AND BRUSHES

Most carvers use acrylic paints; however, many of the top carvers also use oils. The perched hummingbird project will be painted with acrylics; the hovering hummingbird will be painted with oils. Acrylics dry quicker than oils and are usually put on with several layers or "washes." Oils dry slower, which allows the painter a longer period of time for blending and making corrections. Oils use solvents not required by acrylics. These solvents are toxic and flammable. Constant exposure to them over the long-term may result in adverse health effects for some individuals, so proper ventilation is essential.

The quality of your brushes has a direct effect on your finished product. Keep in mind, painting on textured wood tends to break down the fibers of the brush much more quickly than painting on canvas. Many professionals use rounded pure sable brushes in sizes 000 to numbers 6 or 8. These brushes are fairly expensive and may not be available at many hobby stores. You may have to special order them through an art store or carving catalog. Many brands of inexpensive brushes are available, but you may not be pleased with the results. We pay between $3 and $18 for most of our brushes. Specific brushes used for each project will be described in each chapter.

Chapter Three

Perched Broad-Tail

The broad-tailed hummingbird *(Selasphorus platycercus)* is one of the more common hummingbirds in the western United States, and certainly the most common in Colorado. It is commonly found at hummingbird feeders in any of the mountain communities throughout Colorado. It is most abundant between 6890 and 8366 feet in the wooded transition zone and often into alpine meadows. It winters primarily in the highlands of Mexico.

Broad-Tailed Hummingbird Pattern

Figure 3:1 *Broad-tailed hummingbird pattern.*

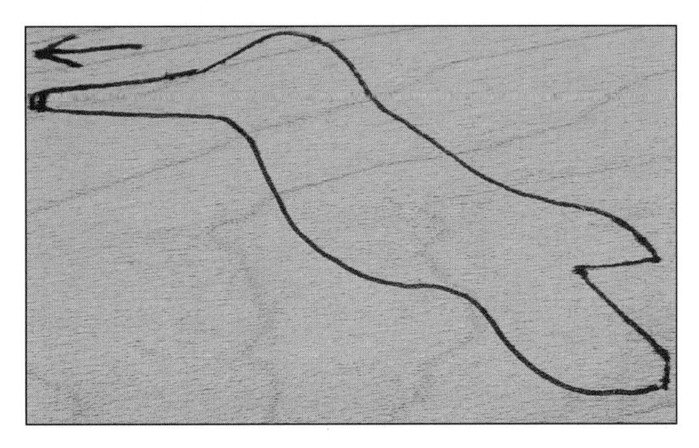

Figure 3:2 *Transfer the pattern to a piece of 3/4-7/8 inch thick basswood. Use a thicker piece of wood if you want to spread the tail wider. Place the bill parallel with the grain of the wood to facilitate carving, even if you decide to insert a copper or brass rod for the bill later.*

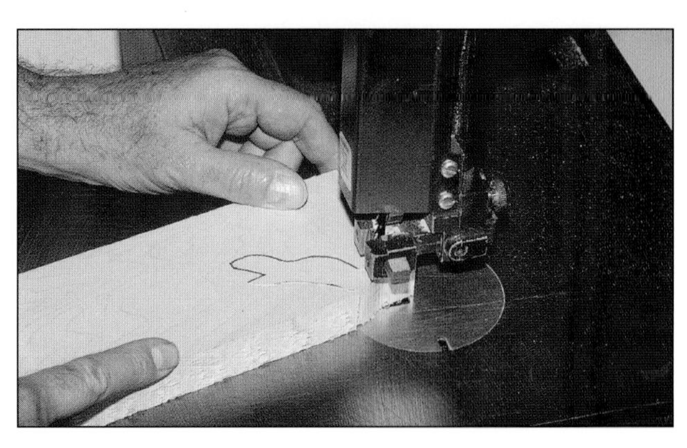

Figure 3:3 *Cut the profile of the bird with a coping or band saw. You don't need to saw the plan or top view because the bird is small.*

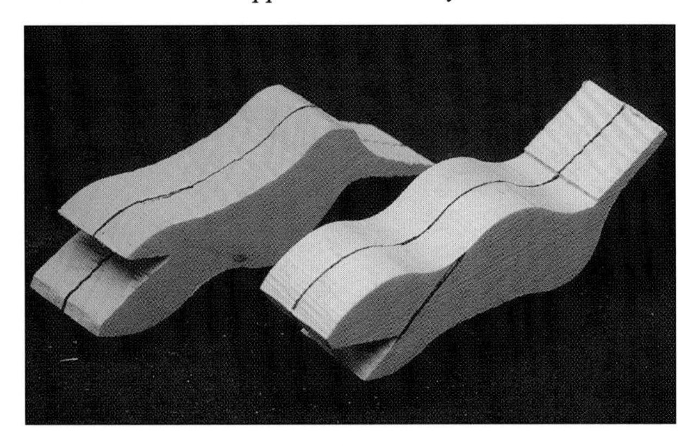

Figure 3:4 *Use a soft lead pencil and draw a center line on the top and underside.*

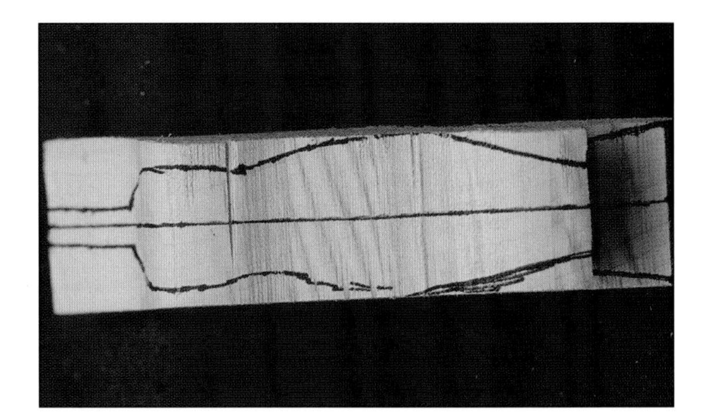

Figure 3:5 *Draw a general plan view. Make the outline oversized-it is easier to take wood off than to add it later!*

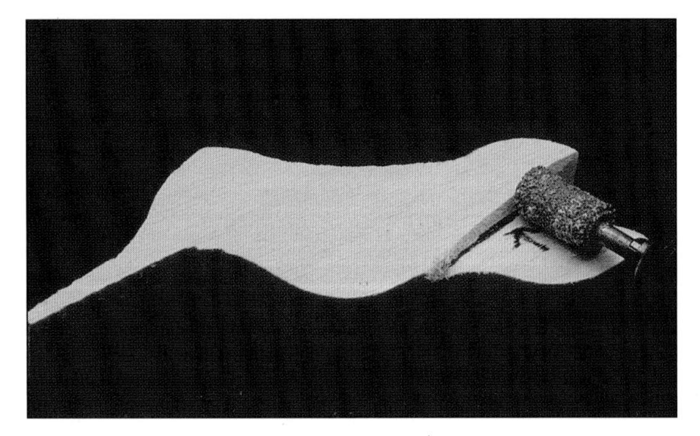

Figure 3:6 *Use a gold cylinder tungsten carbide bit or knife and make a stopcut to define the bottom of the wings and tail on both sides of the blank. (The gold carbide bit is recommended over the silver carbide because the gold leaves a cleaner cut.)*

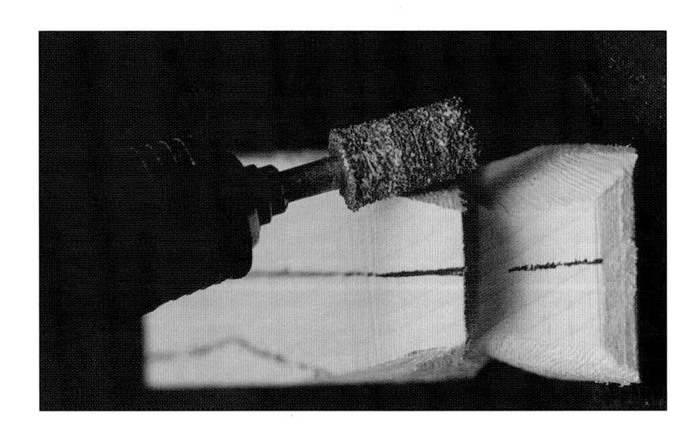

Figure 3:7 *Use the same carbide bit or knife to lightly round or bevel the tail and to bevel the wing tips toward the center line. Remove wood from the back half of the wing area adjacent to the lines drawn on the plan view.*

Figure 3:8 *Follow the plan view and remove wood from the neck, head, and bill areas on both sides using the gold carbide bit or knife. Do not round the bird yet, remove wood vertically to the lines drawn on the plan view.*

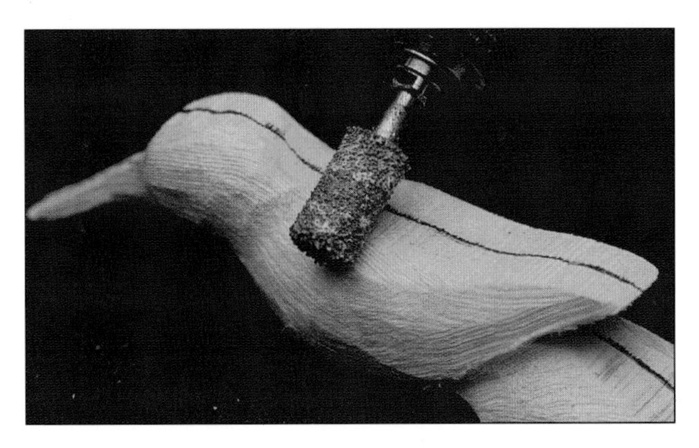

Figure 3:9 *Round the wings and upper back using the gold carbide bit; keep the back 25mm of the wings fairly flat, but beveled from the top to the bottom. Leave 5 mm of wood on both sides of the center line at the wingtips. Round the head, neck, and underside of the belly.*

Figure 3:10 *Create a concave area on the underside of the tail with a rounded gold cylinder. Make it taper gradually from the belly to the end of the tail.*

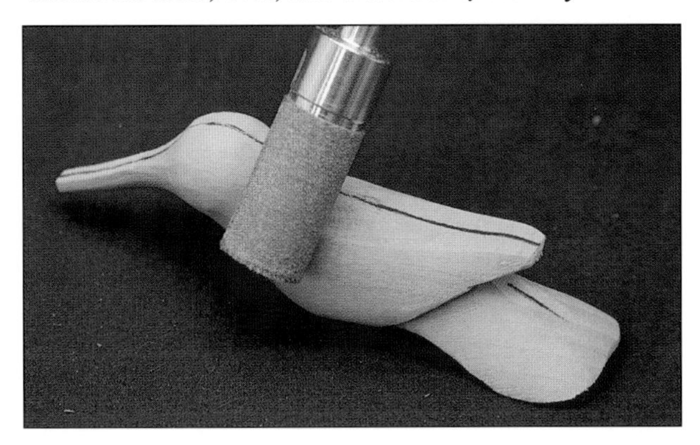

Figure 3:11 *Use a cushioned sanding drum with 150 grit sand paper to smooth the wings, tail, and neck. Continue general shaping during this step. (It will be easier to draw feather patterns on a smooth surface later.)*

Figure 3:12 *Remove wood between the wings using a rotary carbide bit or 1/8-inch gouge. Keep a uniform slope between the body and upper tail coverts. Use caution because it is easy to gouge too deeply when cutting between the wings.* Do not *carve the underside of the primaries to their final width yet-they will be too thin and may break.*

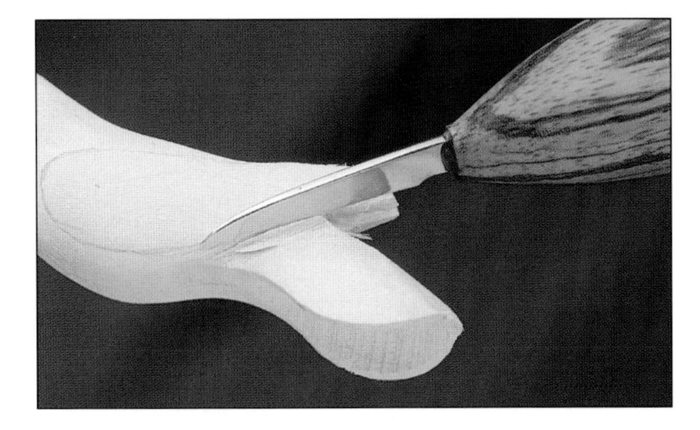

Figure 3:13 *Straighten the area between the primaries and the tail using a knife.*

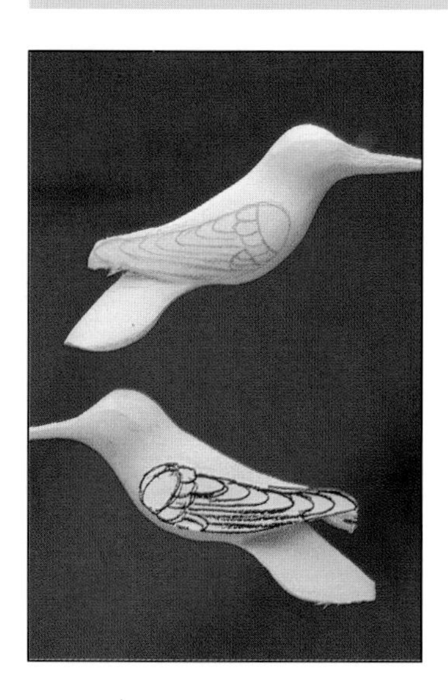

Figure 3:14 *Outline the wings. The wings are about 45 mm long from the tip of the primaries to the shoulder. Draw the scapulars, secondaries, and primaries. Cut the diagram from the pattern and overlay it on the blank. Transfer the pattern to the wood using carbon paper.*

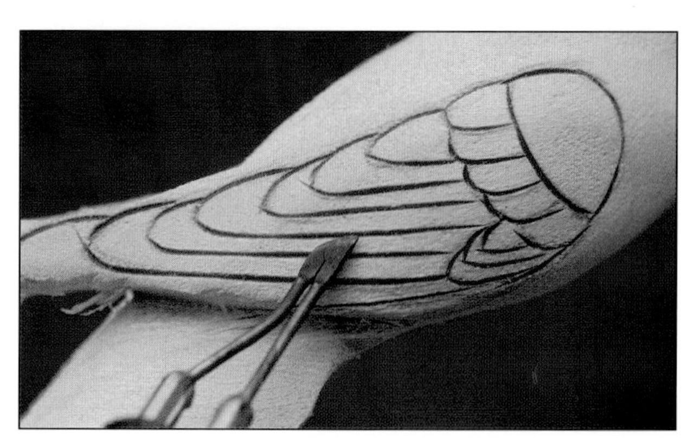

Figure 3:15 *Using a 5/32 inch knife tip burner, outline each of the wing feathers. The burner makes the equivalent of a stopcut.*

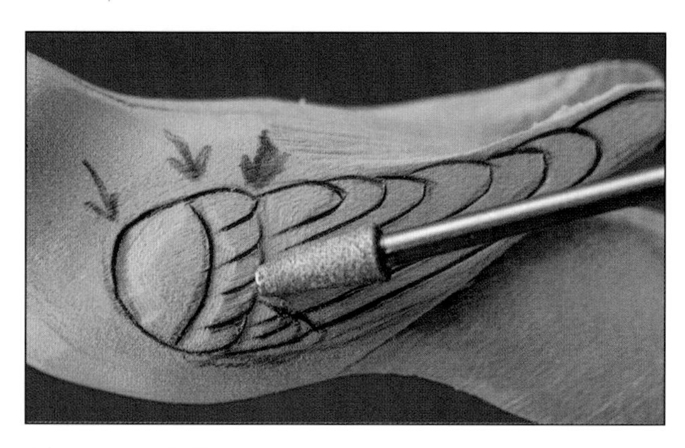

Figure 3:16 *Relieve the front part of the wing using a safe-end diamond or a flame ruby carver; the feathers on the shoulder overlap the wing feathers. Next, relieve the areas between the wing feather groups.*

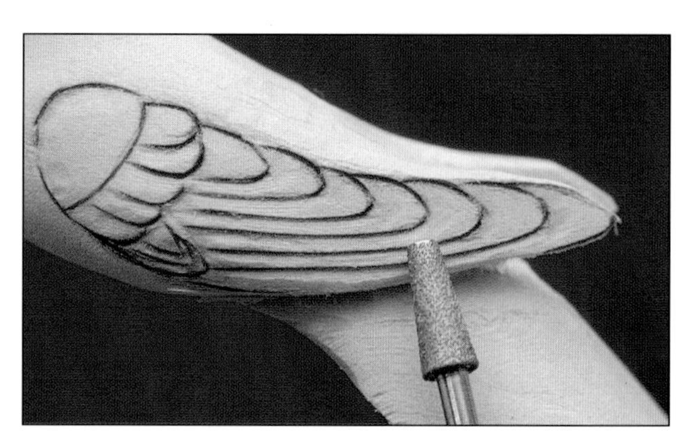

Figure 3:17 *Use a safe-end diamond cylinder or knife to relieve around each secondary. Then relieve around each primary.*

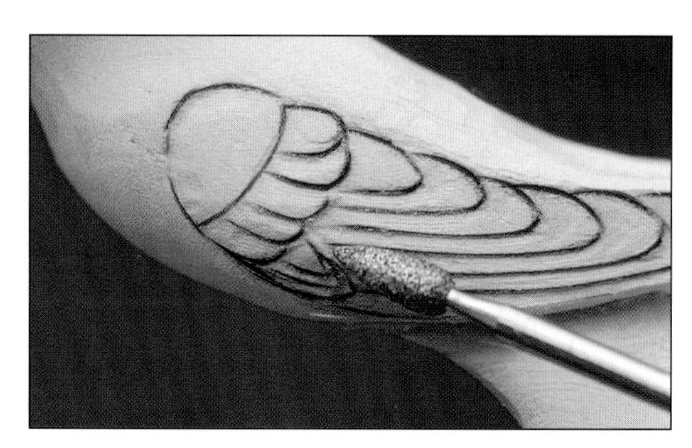

Figure 3:18 *Use the tip of a small flame ruby carver to relieve around feathers in tight groupings, such as the area between the primaries and secondaries.*

Figure 3:19 *Clean the wings using a Scotch defuzzing pad (grey or burgundy; green or brown pads are too aggressive and may remove the detail). This process removes loose particles of wood and smoothes the area.*

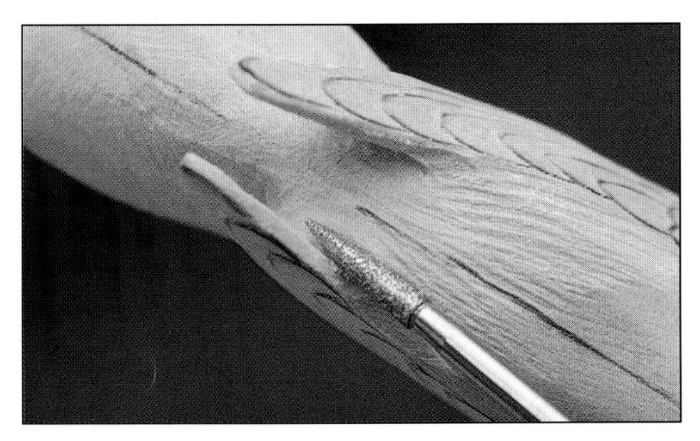

Figure 3:20 *Use a flame ruby carver followed by a spear point diamond to clean the area between the primaries and the lower back and rump. Thin the width of the wings to about 2-3 mm, but not to the final width (approximately 1 mm).*

Figure 3:21 *Trim the excess wood from the top of the wing using a flame ruby carver.*

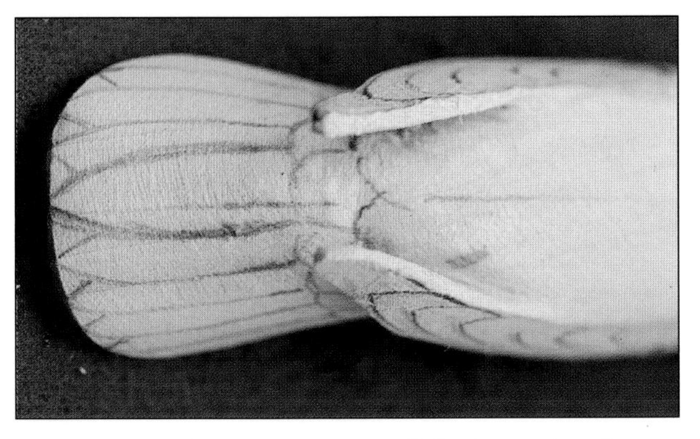

Figure 3:22 *Sketch the upper tail feathers using the pattern. The broad-tailed hummingbird has 10 tail feathers, as do most hummingbirds.*

Figure 3:23 *Burn an outline of the tail feathers using the 5/32 inch knife tip.*

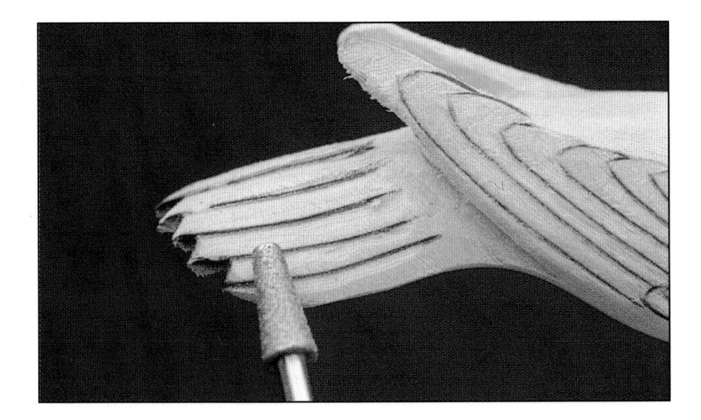

Figure 3:24 *Relieve the tail feathers using a safe edge diamond or knife. Clean the area using the defuzzing pad.*

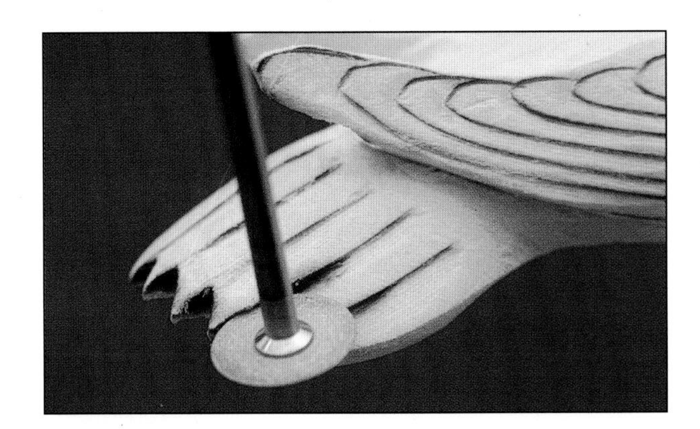

Figure 3:25 *Separate one or two of the tail feathers using the woodburner or a diamond disc. A separation near the outer tip of the tail, about 6-8 mm long, adds interest and realism to the carving.*

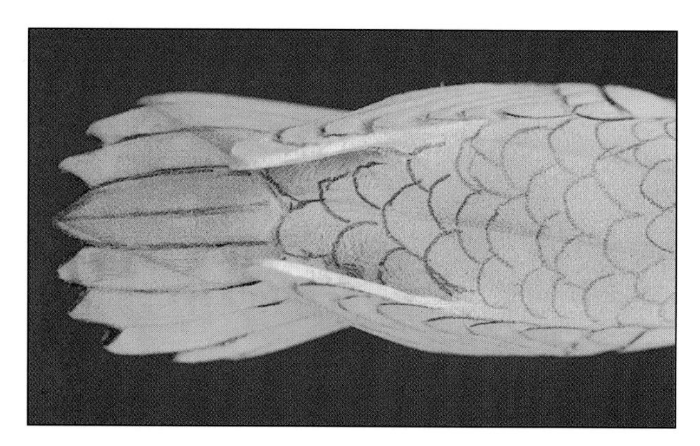

Figure 3:26 *Sketch the upper tail coverts, feathers between the wings, and feathers on the back. The feathers are largest near the tail and become progressively smaller toward the neck and head.*

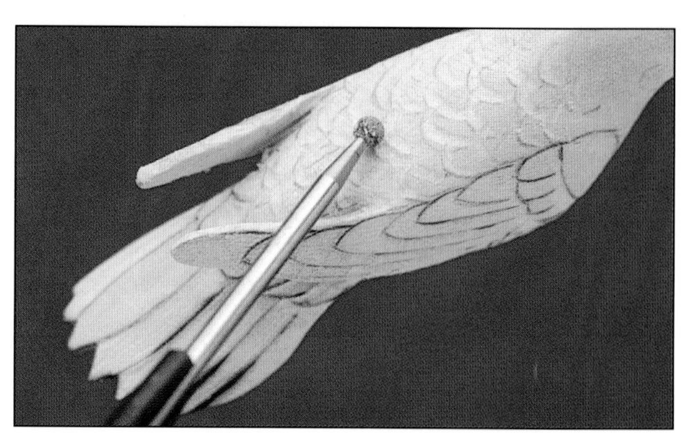

Figure 3:27 *Make a shallow channel around each of these feathers using a small ball diamond or green stone. Lightly round over each edge with the same bit or a tapered green stone. Sand lightly with 220 grit sandpaper.*

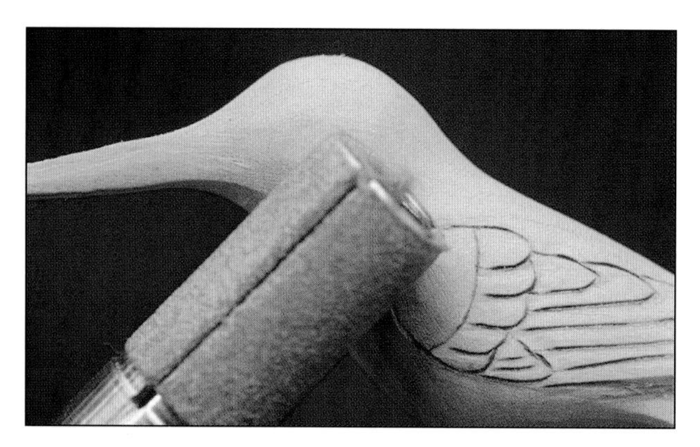

Figure 3:28 *Move to the head. The width of the top of the head is approximately 12 mm at its widest point behind the eye. The width of the head tapers from behind the eye forward to the bill. Use a cushioned drum sander to obtain the general shape.*

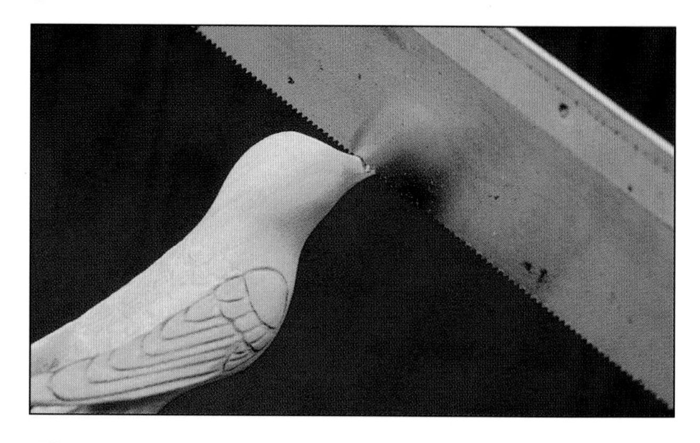

Figure 3:29 *To insert the bill, cut off the wooden bill using an X-acto or another fine-tooth saw. A square, clean cut is desired. A 1/16 inch brass rod is nearly identical to the cross sectional dimension of the broad-tailed hummingbird bill. Carving a bill to this diameter without breaking it is very difficult.*

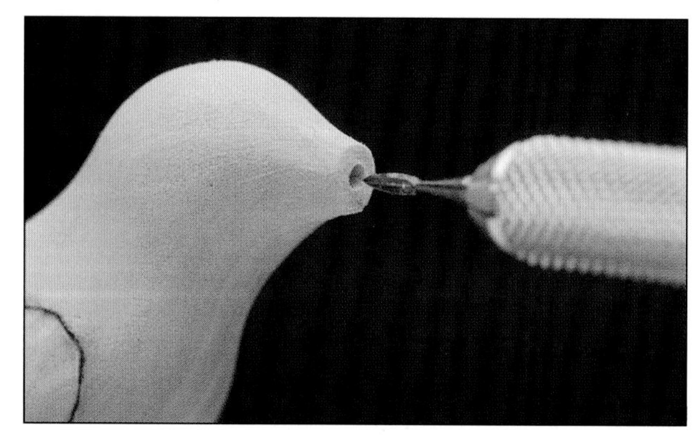

Figure 3:30 *Drill a starter hole using a small pointed stump cutter or small tapered drill in a pin vise.*

Figure 3:31 *Use a 1/16 inch drill to enlarge the hole. Align the drill with the center line on the head. Drill the hole about 5-8 mm into the head.*

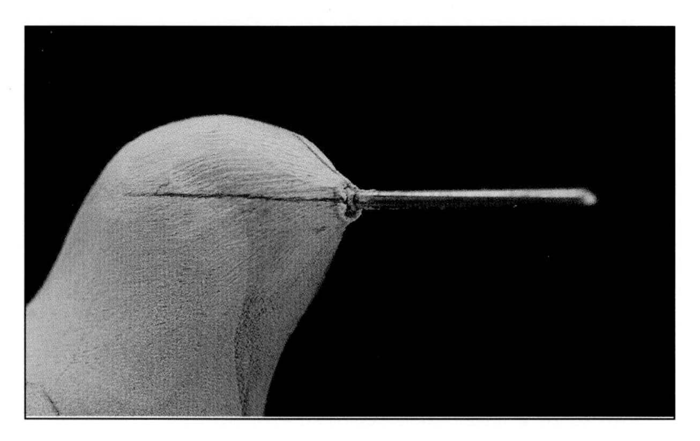

Figure 3:32 *Insert a 1/16 inch brass rod and view it from the top, bottom, and both sides. If it does not line up correctly, make appropriate adjustments.*

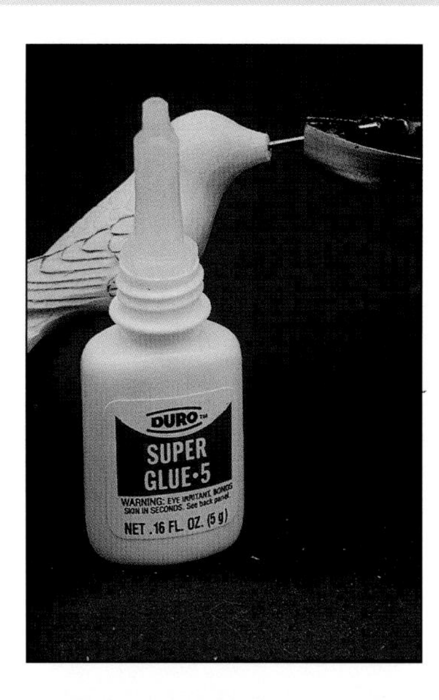

Figure 3:33 *Place a couple drops of super glue on the brass rod and in the hole you just drilled. Insert the rod into the hole, using a pair of pliers to push it into the wood. If you push too hard, the rod may be forced through the back of the neck*–be careful!

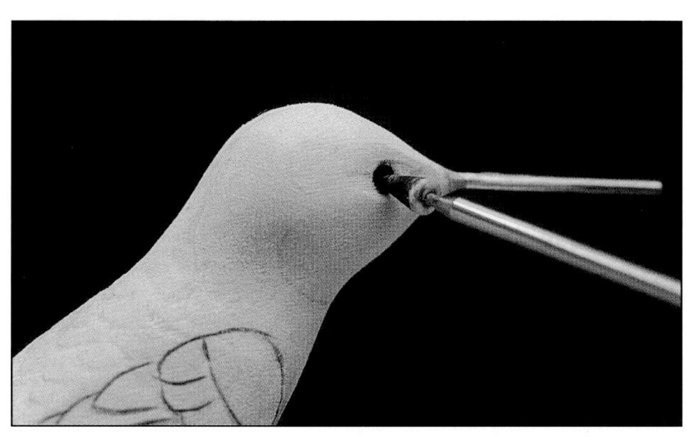

Figure 3:34 *The eye is even with the back of the mouth. The bottom of the eye is even with the commissure line of the bill. When you have aligned the eye location on both sides, insert a pointed instrument in the wood to mark the center of the eye hole. Drill the hole for the eye using a small bullet shaped pink stone or a tapered steel cutter. The eye diameter is 3 mm.*

Figure 3:35 *Cut a channel from the beak to behind the eye using a round ruby carver. The head should be close to final shape. "Fine tune" as necessary.*

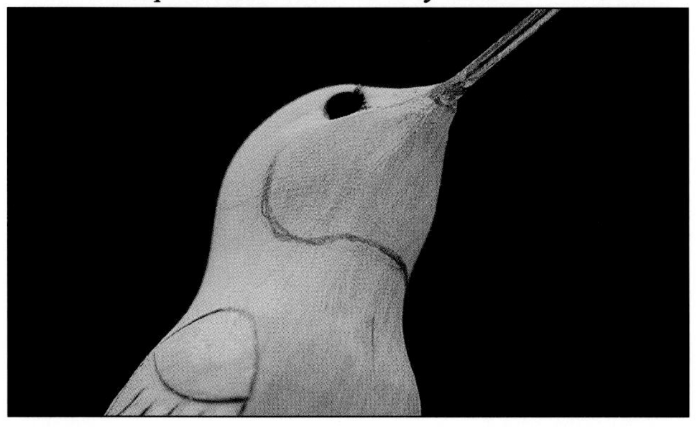

Figure 3:36 *Sketch the general area of the gorget using the pattern as a reference.*

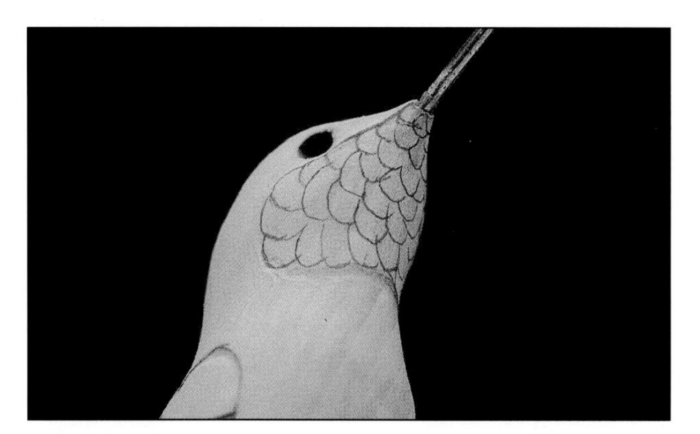

Figure 3:37 *Draw individual feathers on the gorget. The feathers closest to the bill are the smallest; they gradually increase in size near the back of the gorget.*

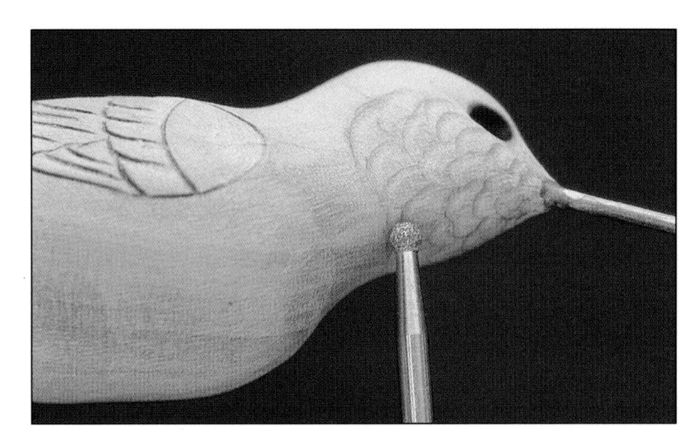

Figure 3:38 *Outline the gorget feathers with the 5/32 inch burner tip or a small round diamond. Contour them with the same round diamond or bullet shaped green stone and sand lightly using 220 grit sandpaper.*

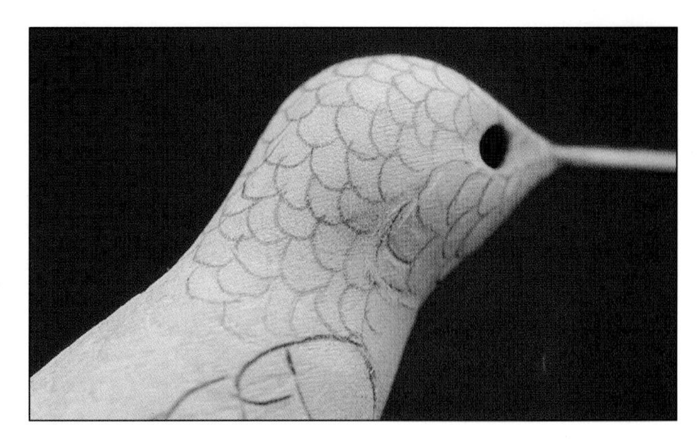

Figure 3:39 *Sketch the feathers on the head. They are smallest near the bill and become larger toward the back of the head. The size of the feathers between the head and back of the neck should be approximately the same. Adjust the size if necessary.*

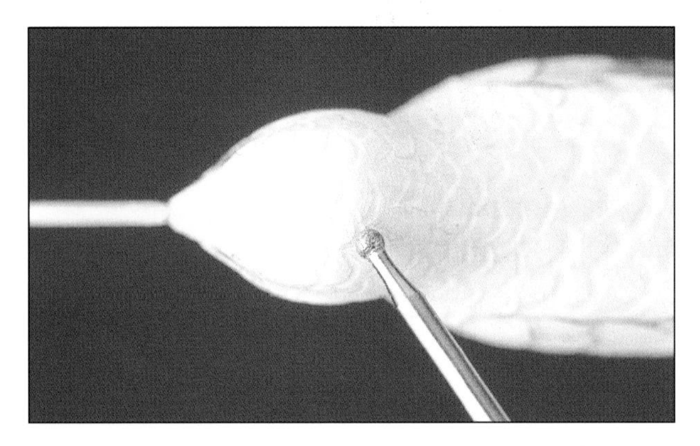

Figure 3:40 *Outline the individual feathers using a small round diamond or green stone. Contour the feathers using a round diamond or green stone, and then sand lightly using 200 grit sandpaper.*

Figure 3:41 *Resketch the feathers on the head to help define them prior to burning.*

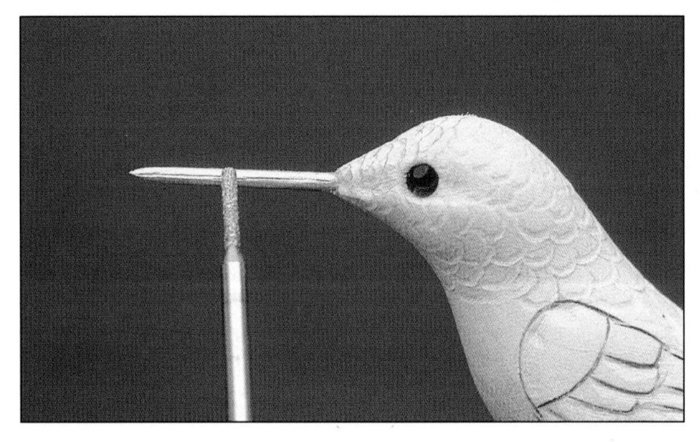

Figure 3:42 *The exposed culmen (bill) is approximately 17.5 mm. Cut the excess from the brass rod with wire cutters and taper the bill using sandpaper or a cut-off wheel. Do not sand for too long at a time because sanding may cause the rod to heat and the hot rod may loosen the super glue and the rod. The line between the upper and lower mandibles (commissure line) can be made with a carbide cutter or diamond bit. Alternatively, you can paint the line.*

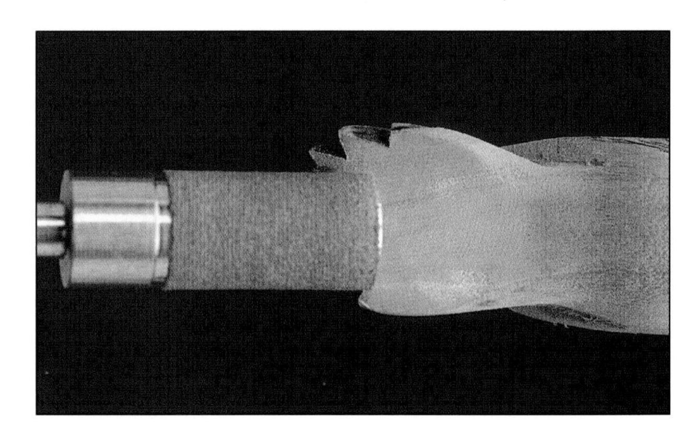

Figure 3:43 *Thin and smooth the underside of the tail and under tail coverts using a cushioned drum sander.*

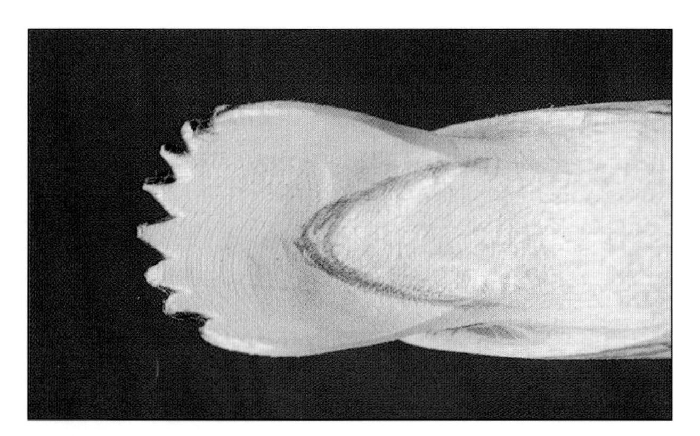

Figure 3:44 *Sketch the general area where the under tail coverts join the tail feathers, and cut a channel between the tail and under tail coverts using a round ruby carver.*

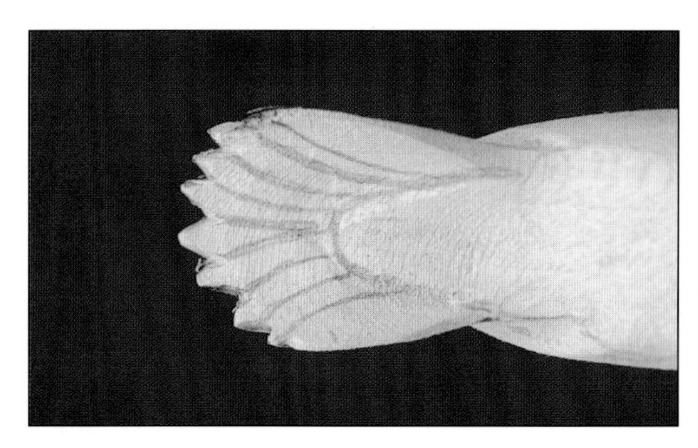

Figure 3:45 *Draw the under tail feathers. The outer feathers on both sides should be a full feather and should meet the tip of the upper tail feather (see pattern). If you have 10 feathers showing on top, 10 should be drawn on the underside.*

Figure 3:46 *Burn and relieve the tail feathers.*

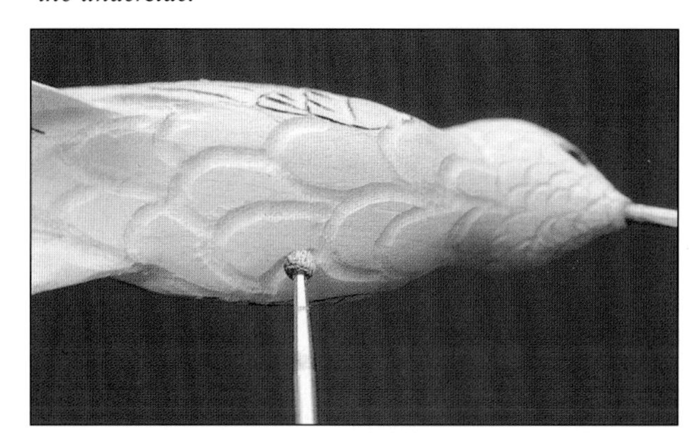

Figure 3:47 *On hummingbirds, there are feather tracts or groups of feathers that give the appearance of high and low areas or "lumps and bumps." Lumps and bumps are not as apparent or exaggerated on a hummingbird as on larger birds. To develop this look on the hummingbird, sketch flowing lines on the under tail coverts, belly, and breast. If you are carving a fat (torpid) hummingbird, it is also desirable to contour the back and mantle of the bird.*

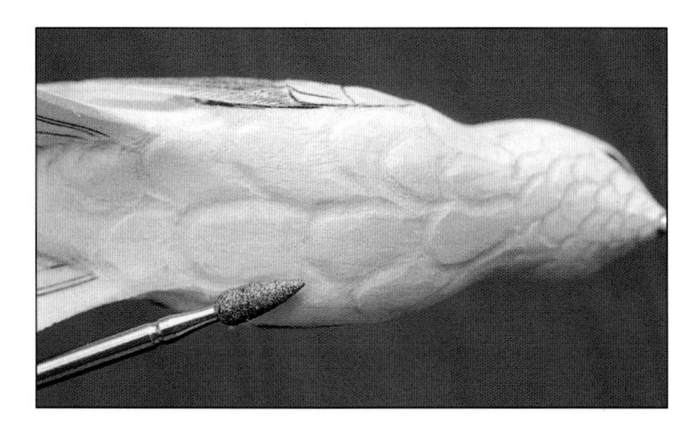

Figure 3:48 *Contour the feather tracts using a flame ruby carver. Each tract should be rounded. Then use the defuzzing pad to clean and smooth the area.*

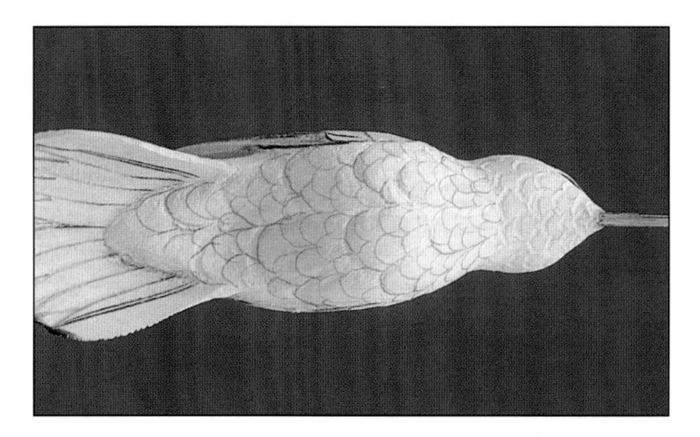

Figure 3:49 *Sketch individual feathers within the tracts.*

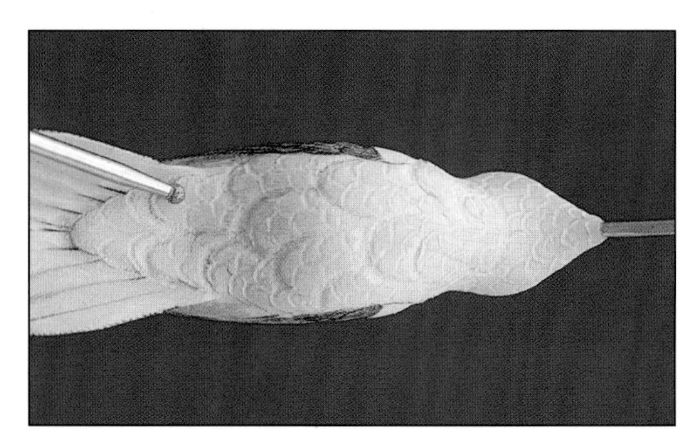

Figure 3:50 *Shape and contour each feather using a round diamond or green stone.*

Figure 3:51 *Sketch and burn both sides of each quill on the primaries, secondaries, wing coverts, and tail feathers. Keep the burn lines close together. Next, lay the burner on its side and burn lightly adjacent to the quill lines. This lowers the area next to the quills and appears to raise the quill.*

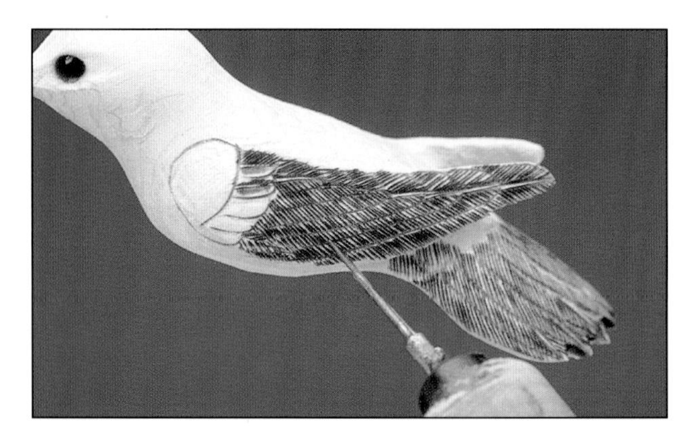

Figure 3:52 *Burn barbs on the primaries, secondaries, wing coverts, and tail feathers using the 5/32 inch knife tip burner. The barb lines are at an angle from the quill and curved. Don't draw the barbs perpendicular to the quills.*

Figure 3:53 *Burn barbs in the wing coverts, head, and gorget feathers.*

Figure 3:54 *Shape and thin the inside of the wings, and burn the barbs.*

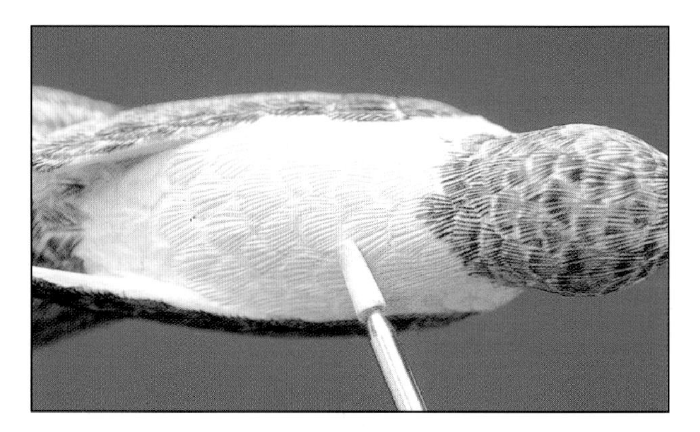

Figure 3:55 *Use a white cylinder stone to texture the feathers on the back, under tail coverts, belly, and chest. The barb lines should be fan shaped and curved.* Do not burn straight or parallel lines.

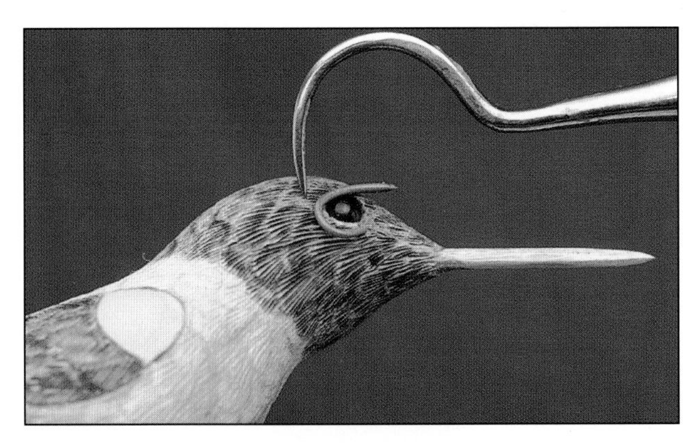

Figure 3:56 *Mix some two-part ribbon epoxy and roll it to make a thin string. Shape it around the eye using a dental tool to form the eye ring and let it dry overnight. The enlarged photo at the left shows a close-up of a broad-tailed hummingbird. Note the placement of and ring around the eye.*

Figure 3:57 *Clean the bird using a rotary brush or medium bristled tooth brush. Your bird is ready to be painted.*

Figure 3:58 *Hummingbirds have very small feet and frequently they are not visible when the bird is perched because they are covered by breast feathers. I chose not to put feet on this carving. Drill a 1/16 inch hole in the lower belly where the bird will be attached to a branch or vine. Insert a 1/16 inch brass rod or spring steel wire into the hole with super glue. Insert the rod or wire into a pin vise to form a holding structure for painting.*

Painting a Broad-Tailed Hummingbird

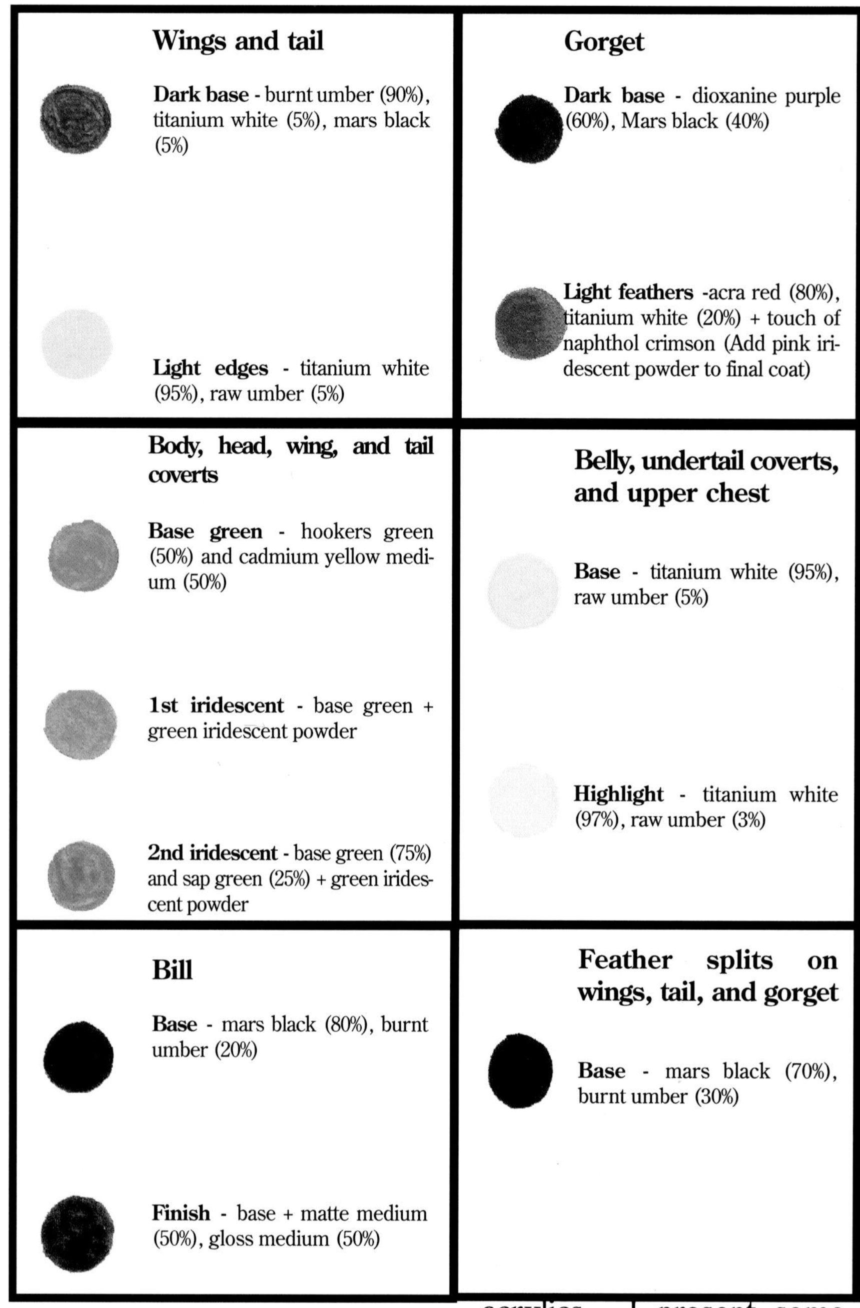

Carvers differ more about painting techniques than about any other aspect of bird carving. Some carvers prefer oils and others prefer acrylics. I present some suggestions that work and know that you will modify them as you gain experience.

Most carvers who paint using acrylics seal their carvings with sanding sealer/lacquer thinner or various sprays prior to painting. Similarly, most carvers use one or more coats of gesso to provide a base of uniform white color and to enhance adhesion of the acrylic paints.

For the perched bird I apply sealer and then gesso. I use Liquetex acrylic paints, a number 4 filbert, number 1 liner, number 10 flat scrubber, and number 3 round sable. All paint is applied as washes. A wash is a small amount of paint mixed with water. The consistency of the mixture approximates 2 percent milk. However, some washes are even thinner. Several washes are required to obtain the finish desired. I dry each wash with a hair dryer.

I suggest relative proportions of each paint to achieve a specific color. You must use judgment on the final percentages because paints vary by manufacturer and by lot number. Also remember that acrylic paints get somewhat darker as they dry. Use the color chart, Figure 3:59, to assist you in obtaining a desired color. Painting is an art and not a science.

Figure 3:59 *Color mixing guide for broad-tailed hummingbird. Acrylic paints used for painting the broad-tailed hummingbird are: raw umber, raw sienna, burnt umber, titanium white, cadmium yellow medium, mars black, hookers green, sap green, dioxinine purple, naphthol crimson, acra violet, green iridescent powder, and pink iridescent powder.*

Figure 3:60 *Clean the bird using a medium-to-soft rotary or medium bristle tooth brush. Spray it with Deft semi-gloss clear wood finish or clear acrylic sealer or paint it with a 50:50 mixture of lacquer thinner and sanding sealer. Let it dry for 10-15 minutes. Repeat, let dry and clean with a brush.*

Figure 3:61 *Use a stiff bristle brush and apply gesso (do not add water) to the entire bird. Scrub the gesso into the texture to keep from filling the texture lines. Let it air dry and repeat 1-2 times. You should be able to see the texture, but not brown or charred black colors from burning.*

Figure 3:62 *Clean the eye using a toothpick, dental tool, or an X-acto knife. Avoid damage to the eye ring.*

Figure 3:63 *Refer to Figures 1:2 and 1:3 and any other reference photographs you have. The Tyrrell book has great photos. Photos are essential if you don't have access to a study skin. The base coat for the belly, undertail coverts, and upper chest area (under the gorget) is a mixture of titanium white and raw umber (95:5). Use 3-4 washes of the mixture.*

Figure 3:64 *Add additional titanium white or gesso to lighten the area under the gorget. Use the lighter mixture and lighten the feather edges of the feathers on the belly, undertail coverts, and chest. Repeat this step 2-3 times. Either fan your brush or use a liner brush and paint around the outside edge. A mixture that is too thin will move through the feather texture into the surrounding area. If it is too thick, it will make a noticeable line and appear artificial.*

Figure 3:65 *Prepare the base coat for the head, back, wing coverts, secondaries, upper tail coverts, and two middle tail feathers using a mixture of hookers green and cadmium yellow medium (50:50). Repeat 2-3 times. Use a clean, wet brush and paint a line of water where the green of the back will meet the white of the breast. Then apply the green mixture to the line. The green will bleed into the water line softening the transition between the two colors. Repeat 3-4 times.*

Figure 3:66 *Apply cadmium yellow medium to the middle of the feathers of the secondaries and several feathers in the center of the head and back. These feathers will be lighted most directly by the sun. Refer again to Figures 1:2 and 1:3. Repeat once or twice.*

Figure 3:67 *Add a small amount of green iridescent powder to a 50:50 mixture of the base green and sap green. Apply to the outer feather edges of the head, back, wing coverts, secondaries, upper tail coverts, and the two middle tail feathers. Repeat 2-3 times.*

Figure 3:68 *Add more green iridescent powder and water to this mixture and wash over the green area. This process blends the green and darkens it slightly. Repeat once if necessary. You should still see a darker feather edge and lighter center in each green feather now.*

Figure 3:69 *Apply a mixture of dioxinine purple and mars black (60:40) to the gorget. Repeat 2-3 times. The gorget will appear black when you finish this step. Most of the center of the gorget will remain dark because it is not directly exposed to the sun.*

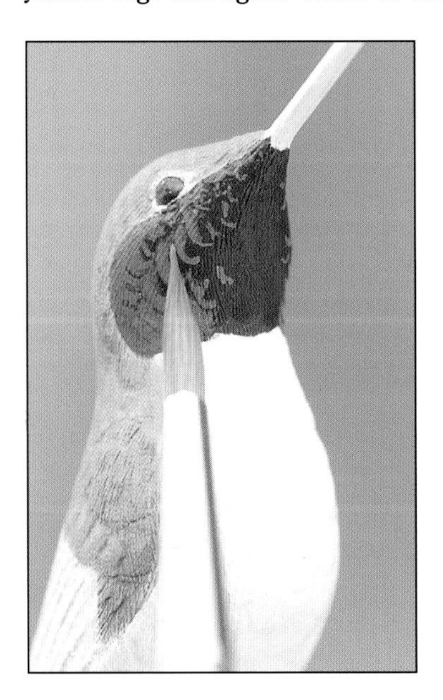

Figure 3:70 *Mix acra violet and white (80:20), plus a small amount of naphthol crimson. Apply to the outer gorget feathers; those feathers where the sun will hit most directly. Not all of the feather is painted (refer to Figures 1:2 and 1:3). Repeat 2-3 times.*

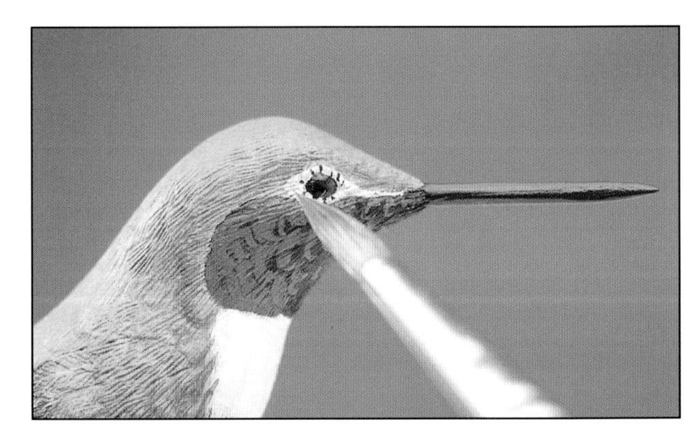

Figure 3:71 *Add some pink iridescence powder to the above mixture and wash across the gorget feathers painted in the previous step. Repeat 2-3 times.*

Figure 3:72 *Mix burnt umber, mars black, and titanium white (90:5:5) for the base color of the wing and tail feathers. Apply this mixture over the front and back sides of the wing and tail feathers, but exclude the two middle tail feathers, which are green. Repeat 3-4 times. Make the insides of the feathers darker than the outside edges by adding a very diluted wash of black to the center part of the primaries and tail feathers if necessary.*

Figure 3:73 *Paint the feather edges of the primaries and the tail feathers using a liner brush or the round sable and a mixture of titanium white and raw umber (95:5). Repeat once if necessary. Mix a small amount of raw umber with a large amount of water (will look like dirty water–only a small amount of pigment and a large amount of water) and apply the wash over the entire wings and tail.*

Figure 3:74 *Mix a dark wash of mars black (70%) and burnt umber (30%) and paint the feather splits in the tail and primaries using a liner or fine tip sable brush.*

Figure 3:75 *Mix a small amount of green iridescent powder to sap green. Apply 3-4 washes to the outside edges of the feathers on the head and back. The darkest feathers will be along the sides because of greater shadowing.*

Figure 3:76 *Use titanium white and raw umber (95:5) to paint the eye ring. Then add small black lines in the grooves around the eye ring.*

Figure 3:77 *Paint the bill using a mixture of mars black and burnt umber (80:20). Repeat 2-3 times. Then apply a mixture of matte medium and varnish (gloss) medium (50:50) to the bill. Repeat 3-5 times.*

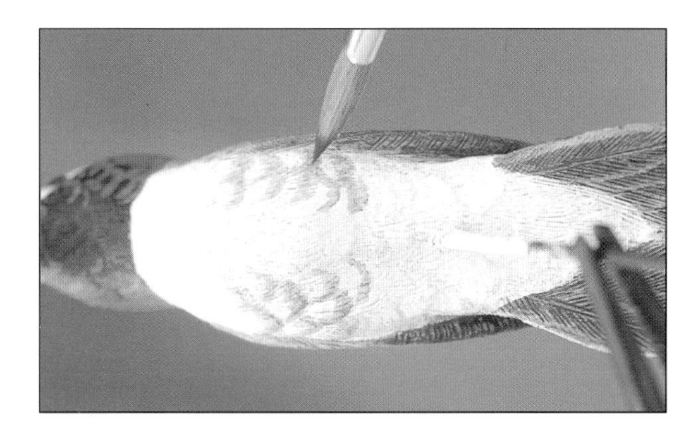

Figure 3:78 *Using the base green mixture (Figure 3:65), apply paint to the outside edges of several feathers on the chest. Repeat 1-2 times. Next, add iridescent green and wash once more. The photo on the left shows a close-up of the coloring on a broad-tailed hummingbird's chest and gorget.*

Figure 3:79 *Dry brush the chest and belly with raw sienna (a small amount of pigment on the brush and lightly brush across the texture line*—this is not a wash*). Repeat once if necessary. After it is dry apply a very diluted wash of raw umber to the chest, belly, under tail coverts, and tail.*

Figure 3:80 *The completed project.*

Chapter Four

Hovering Ruby-Throat

The ruby-throated hummingbird breeds throughout the eastern half of North America where it is found primarily in mixed woodlands and eastern deciduous forests rich in wildflowers (Johnsgard 1983). Ruby-throated hummingbirds forage on at least 31 plant species in their breeding range; the predominant color of most hummingbird-adapted flowers is red (Johnsgard 1983). The ruby-throated hummingbird for this carving is hovering, feeding from a red morning-glory. Several general design concepts were applied when planning this piece. The first concept involved the rule of thirds, a concept that photographers and painters have used for two-dimensional artwork. To apply this rule, imagine that a "frame" that would bound your piece is divided into nine equal areas by two vertical and two horizontal lines (like a tic-tac-toe board). The lines intersect at four points within the "frame." Locating your subject off-center on one of these points will usually be more interesting than if it were stuck exactly in the middle. For this carving, I have located the eye of the hummingbird at one

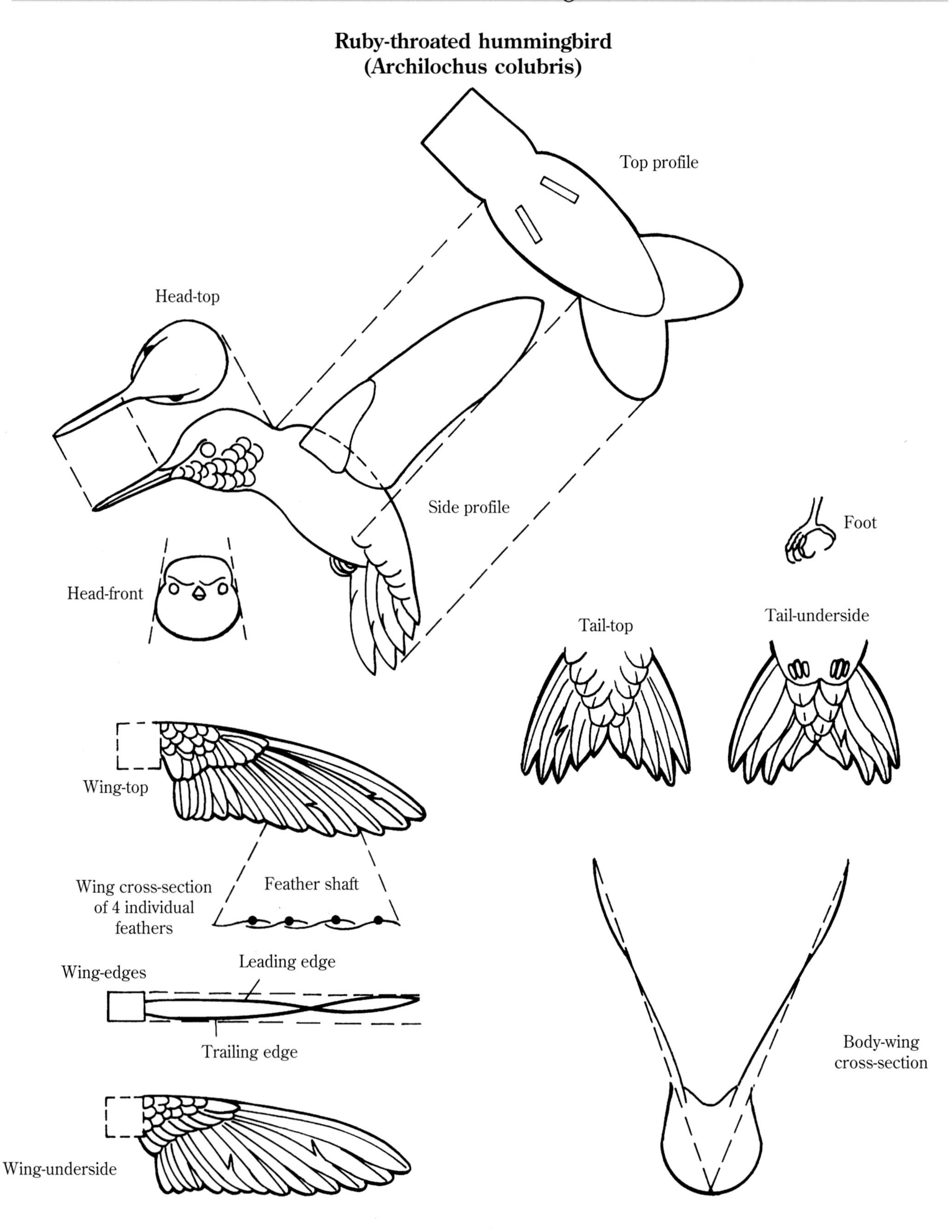

Figure 4:1 *Ruby-throated hummingbird pattern*

of the upper intersection points. Once the main subject was located in the frame, the habitat was designed around it. The concept applied to design of the morning-glory vine involved using s-shaped or c-shaped curves; in this case, the vine has a subtle s-shape. There are many other design concepts that can be applied to bird carvings and their habitat. Many art books have chapters devoted to design and several articles in *Wildfowl Carving and Collecting Magazine* (Mullican 1988, Schroeder 1988) have addressed the subject.

When working on the pattern for a bird in flight, it is important to understand how that bird flies. For example, a hummingbird's wings move in different ways depending on whether it is hovering, flying straight ahead, or backing up. When a hummingbird is hovering, the tips of the wings trace a shallow figure-eight pattern (see Figure 1:5). The wing position in this carving is toward the back of the figure-eight just as the wings have started forward (between Steps 1 and 2). In this position, the wings are starting to turn over; there is only a small amount of twist along the length of each wing (as compared to Step 7 in Figure 1:5) and the tips are just starting to flare backwards. With the wings up like this, the scapular feather groups "bulge" out somewhat. If you were carving the wings in a different position while the bird is hovering, or were carving the bird as if it were backing up or flying forward, the twist along each wing, the flare of the tips, and the bulge of the scapulars should be adjusted accordingly. The pattern for this carving is shown in Figure 4:1.

Before starting the bird carving, however, it is suggested that you go to Chapter 6 and build the morning-glory vine and its base. Several of the following carving and painting steps (making the bill, painting highlights and shadows) require that the bird be temporarily mounted in the flower.

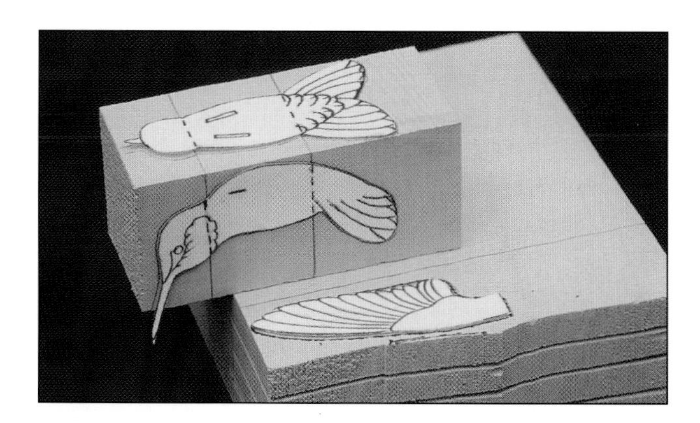

Figure 4:2 *Trace the side and top body profile patterns on a 2 1/2" x 1 1/2" x 1 1/2" block of tupelo (or basswood). Note that the patterns for cutting the blank include only a part of the beak, which will be made from 1/16" diameter spring steel rod later. Be sure to orient the top and side patterns correctly, making sure that the reference lines connecting the two patterns are straight up and down (for the side profile) and straight across (for the top profile) on your blank. Trace the wing pattern on two pieces of tupelo at least 1/4" thick (I have cut slots in the wood so I can cut out multiple wings at a time).*

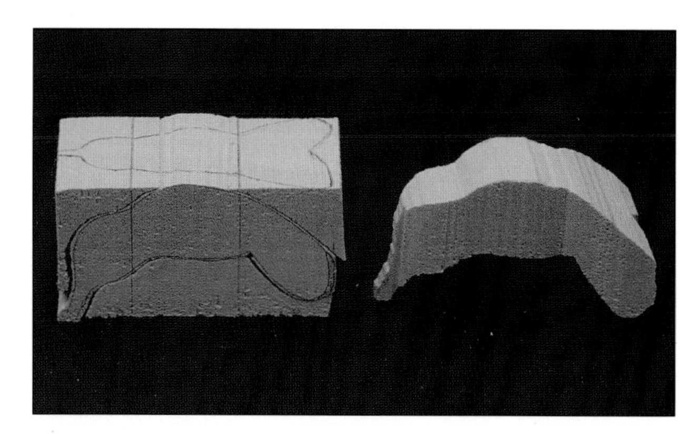

Figure 4:3 *Cut the blanks out on a bandsaw. Be sure to cut on the lines and not outside the lines; otherwise your blank will be too big. For the body, start by cutting the side profile. Next, temporarily glue the top and bottom pieces back on the blank with a small drop of glue from a hot glue gun. This will keep the blank in the correct position when cutting the top profile. Now cut the top profile. Finally, pry the top and bottom pieces from the body and scrape off any remaining hot glue.*

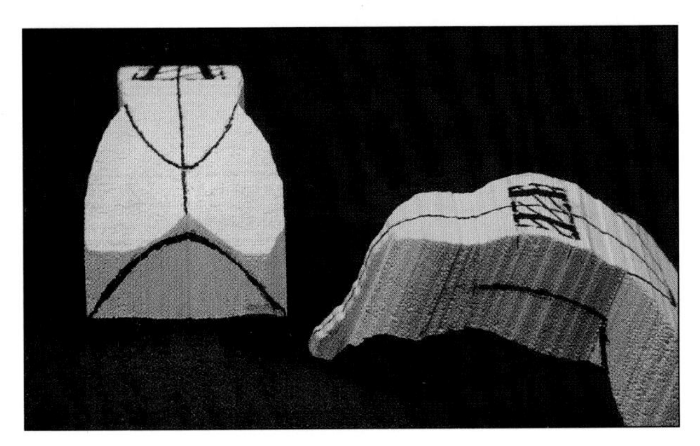

Figure 4:4 *Draw a centerline on the top, bottom, and both sides of the body blank. Do* not *cut into the centerline as you are roughing out the blank or you will change the side profile! On the top of the blank, mark the wing insertion slots and draw crosshatches between the slots and 3mm on either side of the slots. This area will remain flat during roughout; it will be shaped into scapular feathers (on the top) and axillar feathers (on the bottom) when the wings are inserted. Sketch the lines that separate the tail feathers from the upper tail coverts on top of the blank and the tail feathers from the lower tail coverts on the bottom of the blank. Note that the upper tail covert area is more rounded and doesn't go as far back on the tail feathers as the lower tail covert area, which is more pointed and almost completely covers the two center tail feathers. Draw a line to extend the outside tail feathers to the body centerline. On the back edge of the tail area, draw a midline corresponding to the curvature of the tail. The amount of curvature is determined from the side pattern; the outside tail feathers are fanned 15mm in front of the center tail feathers, therefore the back midline should have 15mm of curvature.*

Figure 4:5 *Use a small tapered carbide kutzall to cut a groove around the upper tail coverts. The groove should be fairly shallow in back and should extend forward to where the outside tail feather meets the body centerline.*

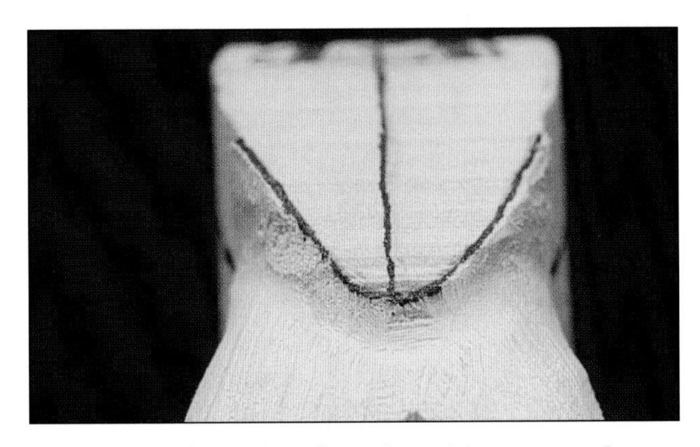

Figure 4:6 *Slope the tail out from this groove to the midline on the back of the tail.*

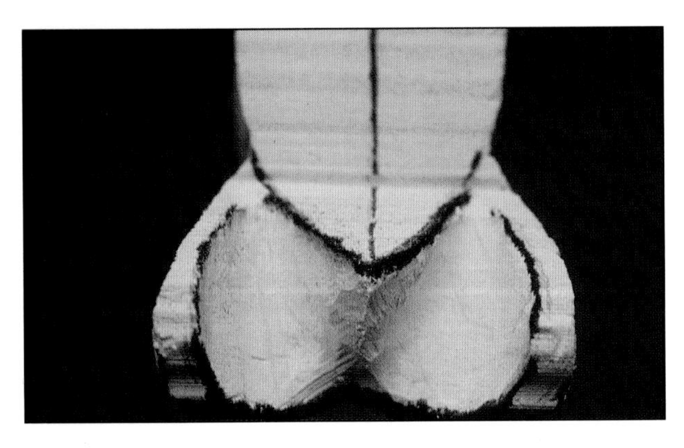

Figure 4:7 *Cut a groove around the lower tail coverts then "hollow" out the underside of the tail to match the top surface. Leave the tail at least 4mm thick for now.*

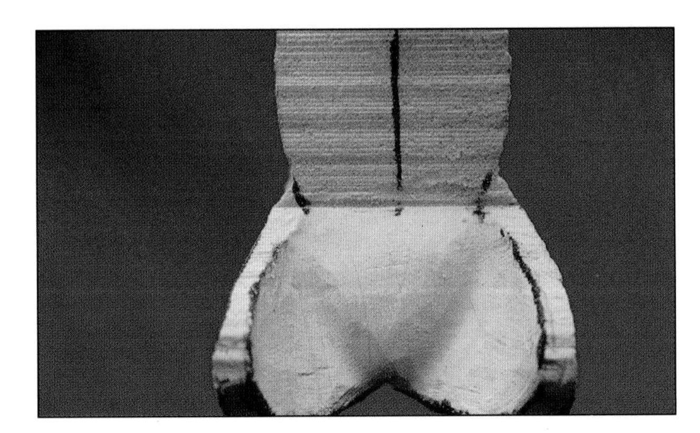

Figure 4:8 *Remove the extra wood from the bottom of the lower tail coverts (so the tail coverts are about 4mm higher than the tail feathers). Round over the upper and lower tail coverts.*

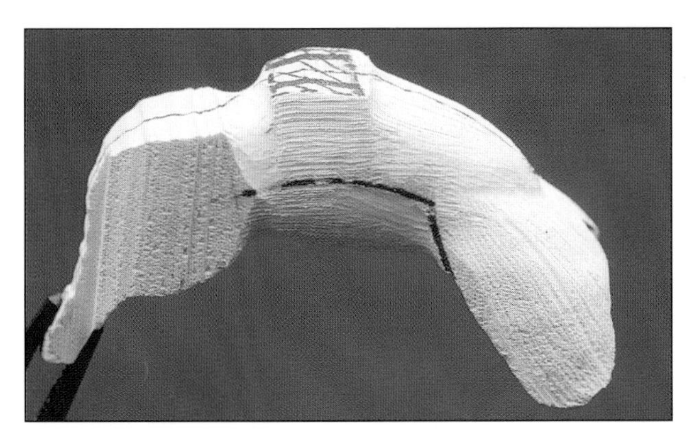

Figure 4:9 *Using a tapered kutzall, rough out the body (but not the cross-hatched area) from the shoulders down to the tail by rounding from the belly centerline up to the side centerlines, and from the top centerline down to the side centerlines. Check to make sure that the maximum body width matches the pattern.*

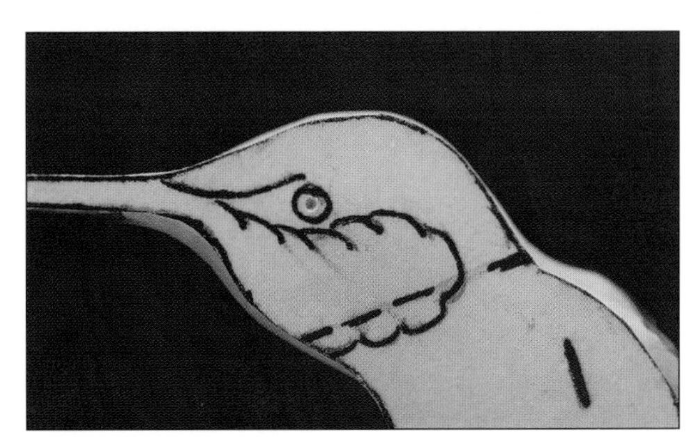

Figure 4:10 *Next, rough out the head. The head is the most important part of the bird; it is what most people look at first and it defines the character of the bird. You should therefore spend a lot of time shaping and refining the head. Start by marking the base of the neck in the back, and the bottom of the gorget on the front and sides of the head. When roughing the head, stay above (in front of) these lines or you will be grinding away part of the body. If you left excess wood around the blank when you cut the side profile on the bandsaw, then trace the side profile view of the head on your blank again. Remove any excess wood with the kutzall bit.*

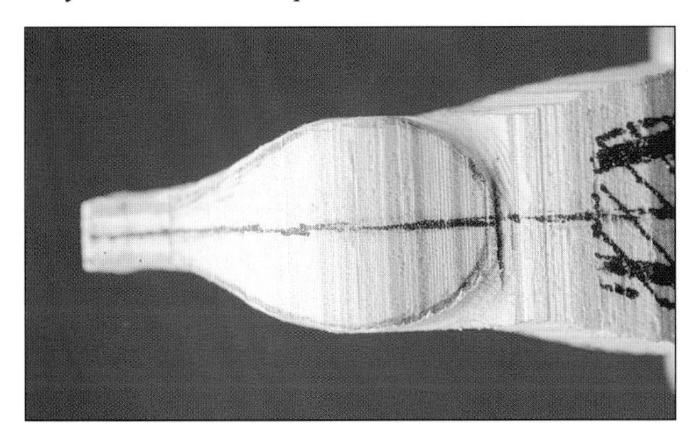

Figure 4:11 *Draw the top view of the head on your blank. Using a small cylindrical kutzall bit, grind away any excess wood, leaving the sides of the head straight up and down for now.*

Figure 4:12 *When the top profile is correct, look at the head from the front. Note on the pattern that the head tapers slightly from bottom to top. Mark the width of the top of the head on your blank (about 12mm) and taper the head with the carbide kutzall bit or a cartridge sanding roll.*

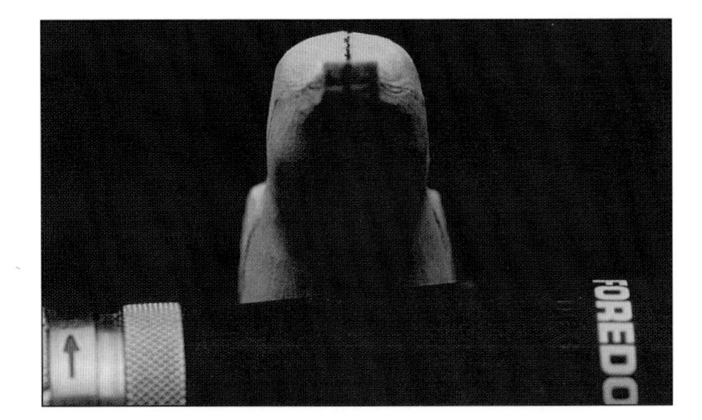

Figure 4:13 *After the top, front, and side profiles are roughed out, round over the sharp edges, but leave the top of the head relatively flat as shown in the front view pattern. Round over the neck area so that the head flows into the back, sides, and breast.*

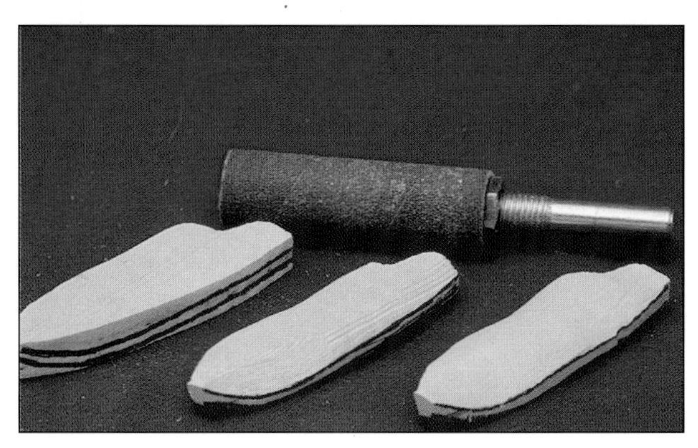

Figure 4:14 *Start roughing out the wings by drawing the leading edge contour (from the front/back wing pattern) on the front of each wing and the trailing edge contour on the back of each wing. Draw lines 2mm on either side of the leading edge contour and the trailing edge contour. Be careful when drawing these contours on your blanks; it is easy to end up with two right or two left wings. The pattern shows the left wing contours as viewed from the front of the wing, and the right wing contours as viewed from behind the wing. To check, hold the wings in place; the tips should both curve slightly up at the end. If one of the wing tips curves out instead of up, you have the contours upside down on that blank. Using a sanding sleeve, shape the leading and trailing edges of each wing. Do* not *thin the tabs that will be inserted into the body yet. When the edges are correct, connect the front of the wing to the back with smooth curves by removing excess wood from the top surface. The top of the wing towards the leading edge should be somewhat convex (rounded over).*

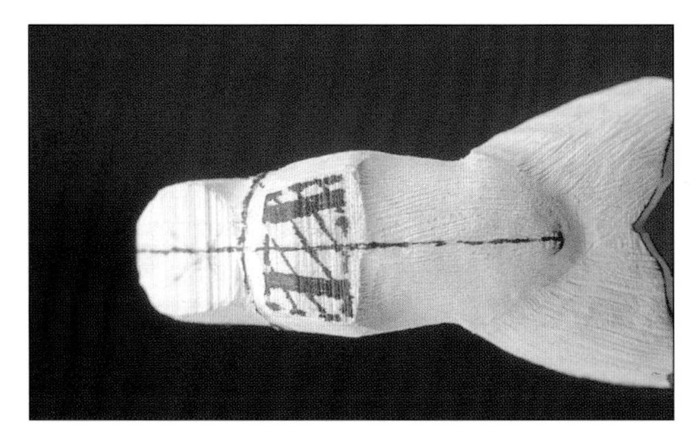

Figure 4:17 *Mark the wing insertion slots on your blank (they should still be visible since we left this area flat during roughout, but they may have been smudged from handling). Using a cylindrical bit, cut a slot 3mm wide by 7mm long and 6mm deep for each wing. To get the correct angle for the slots, lay the pattern of the body cross-section on your bench. Line the carving up with the pattern, line your grinder up with one of the wings, and start cutting the slot. Repeat for the other side.*

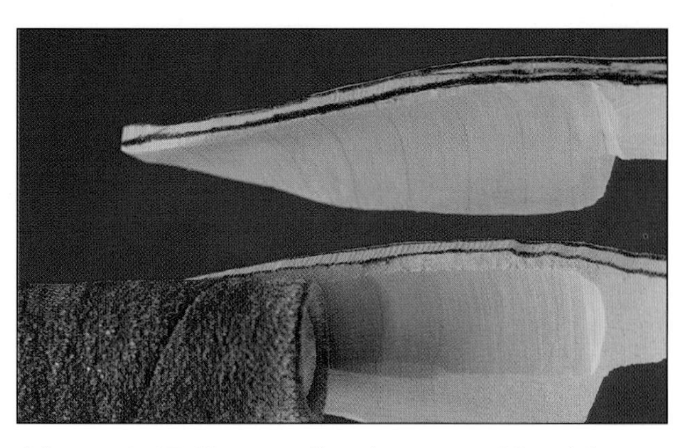

Figure 4:15 *Use a sanding sleeve or cushioned drum sander to connect the leading and trailing edges on the underside of the wing. The underside towards the leading edge should be somewhat concave (dished in). As you shape the underside of the wing to match the top surface, thin the entire wing to about 4mm.*

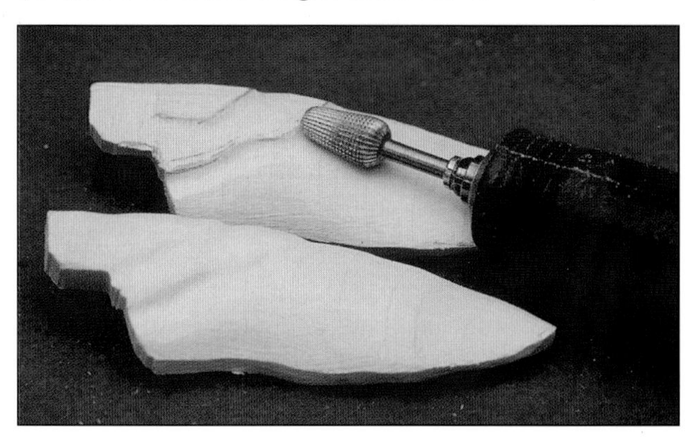

Figure 4:16 *Draw the covert feather groups (middle/lesser, greater) on the top and bottom of each wing. Cut a shallow groove along these lines with the side of a pear-shaped ruby or stump cutter. Smooth the top groove (the one separating the middle/lesser coverts from the greater coverts) out onto the greater covert area, and smooth the bottom groove (separating the greater covert area from the primary/secondary feathers) out to the edges of the wing. Now that you have smoothed out the feathers* below *each groove, round over the feathers* above *each groove. In this photograph, the grooves have been cut in the top wing and have been smoothed out and rounded over on the bottom wing. Finally, sand the wings with 220 or 400 grit sandpaper. I prefer using a cushioned sanding drum for this step but you can also do it by hand.*

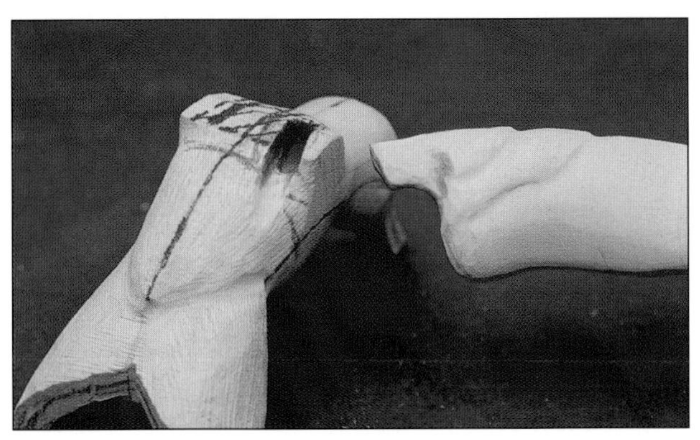

Figure 4:18 *Shape the tab on each wing by thinning the tab to about 4mm thick. To determine where additional wood needs to be removed, blacken the inside of the slot with a soft lead pencil. Insert the tab in the slot and wiggle the wing slightly. Remove the wing. The smudges on the tab indicate where a* small *amount of wood needs to be removed.*

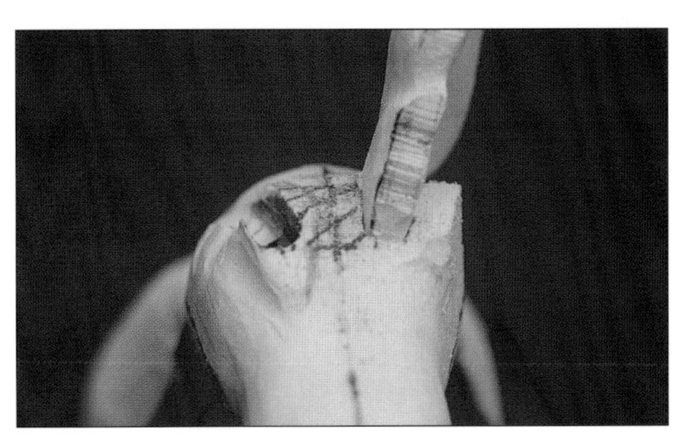

Figure 4:19 *Repeat this process over and over (go slowly) until you get a good tight fit between the wing and body. The better the fit now, the less patching you will have to do later. As the tab starts to fit down into the slot, you will probably have to cut a groove on the back of the flat area to accommodate the secondary wing feathers.*

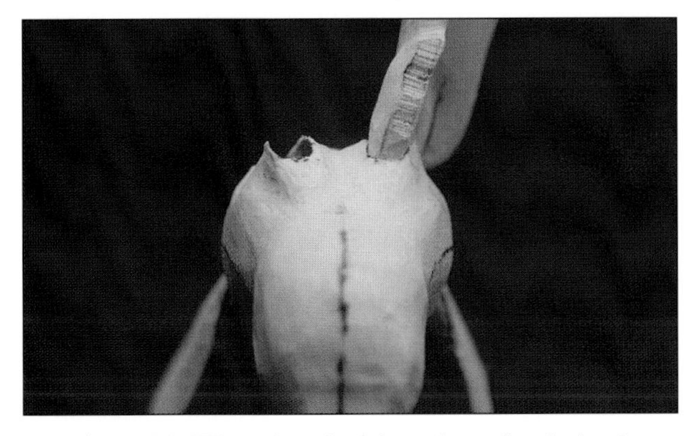

Figure 4:20 *When the wings have been fitted, sketch the scapular feather group in the crosshatched area above each wing, and the axillar feather group below each wing. Note that the scapular group bulges out somewhat when the wings are up. Shape these feather groups with a pear-shaped ruby bit.*

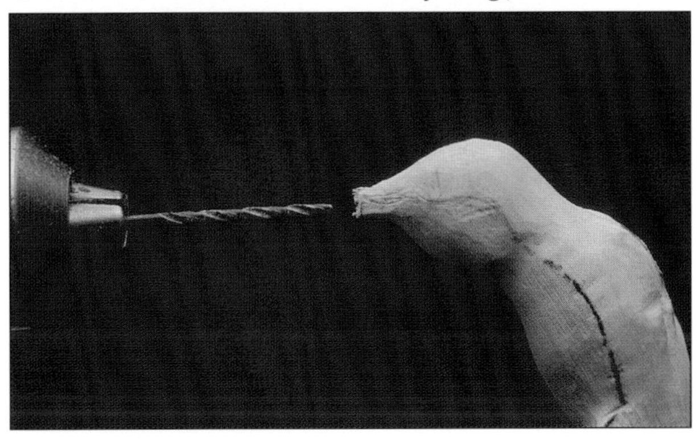

Figure 4:21 *The beak is made from 1/16" piano wire or spring steel rod. Grind away the wooden beak back to the point where the beak meets the forehead and chin feathers. Mark the center of the beak and make a starter hole by pushing a small nail into the mark. Drill a 1/16" hole about 12mm deep, making sure you are going straight into the head.*

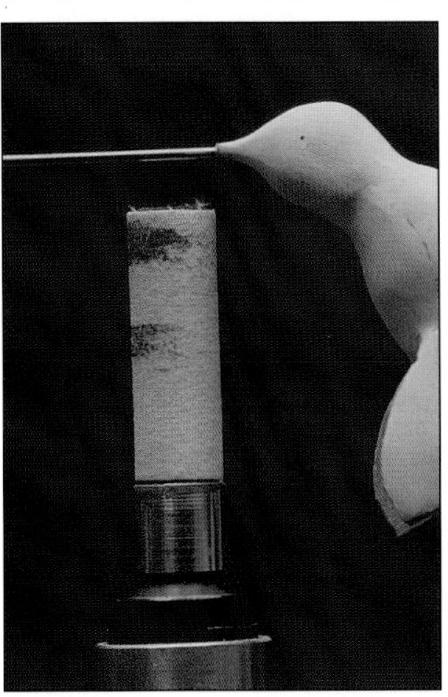

Figure 4:22 *Cut a 55mm length of 1/16" diameter piano wire or spring steel rod, put a drop of 5-minute epoxy on one end, and push that end of the rod into the hole. When the glue has dried, use a cushioned sanding drum to smooth the forehead and chin into the beak.*

Figure 4:23 *Insert the beak of the hummingbird into the copper tube inside the flower the bird is feeding from. Trim the end of the wire with diagonal cutters so that the eyes are about 20mm to 22mm back from the edge of the flower petals. This will put the beak far enough in the flower that it won't be obvious that the wire is much longer than the actual beak length.*

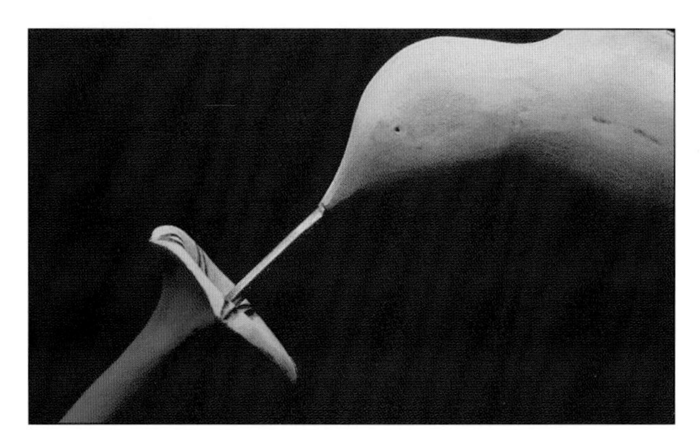

Figure 4:24 *Use a sanding sleeve to make the* top half *of the beak slope down from the top centerline to form a triangular cross-section (Figure 4:1). Complete the roughing out process by sanding the entire bird with 220 grit sandpaper on a cushioned sanding drum.*

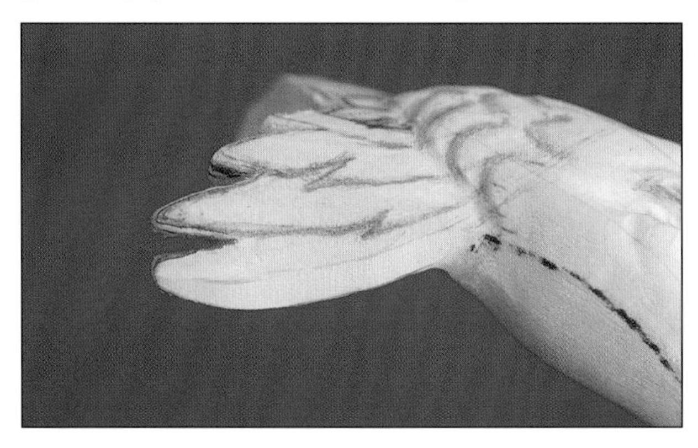

Figure 4:26 *Draw the tail feathers. Sketch feather splits in now. Major splits should be planned in advance because the tip of the split usually extends slightly outside the normal feather edge line. Grind or burn away any excess wood from the feather tips and separations between feather tips and taper the feather edges down to the midline.*

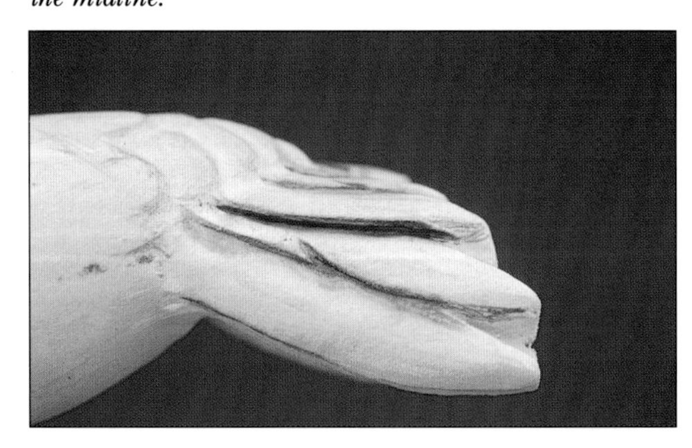

Figure 4:28 *Round over each feather with your grinder. Using a knife-edge burning tip, slightly under cut some of the tail feathers to make them look more separated. Again, use a low heat setting on your burner to avoid charring the wood. Lightly sand each feather with a white stone or 220 grit sandpaper.*

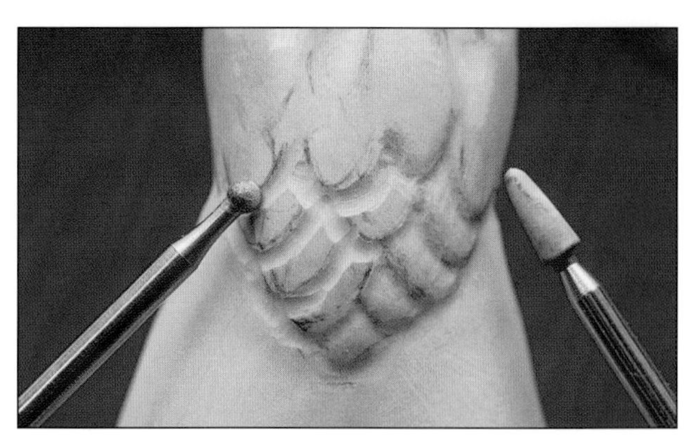

Figure 4:25 *Draw in the individual feathers on the upper tail covert area. Cut a* shallow *groove around each feather using a small ball- or pear-shaped bit (I will be using these shapes in a ruby bit for many of the following steps). We want to give a slightly puffy appearance to these feathers, but they should not bulge out, so keep the groove shallow! For each feather, round over the feather into the groove that defines it, then smooth the groove out onto the feather below it using a white stone with a rounded end (you may have to buy a square-end tapered or cylinder white stone and round over the end yourself using a truing stone or diamond sharpening stick). In this photograph, the feathers on the left have the grooves cut while the feathers on the right have been rounded and smoothed.*

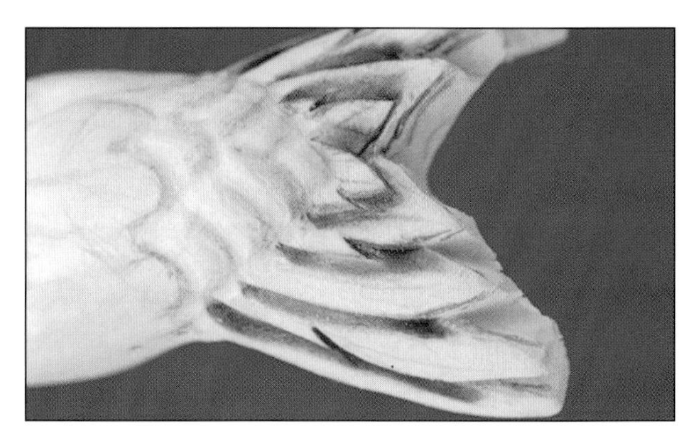

Figure 4:27 *Starting on top in the center of the tail, define the separation between tail feathers by laying a woodburning tip on its side (so the side of the burner is laying on the next lower/outer feather) and drawing it along each tail feather line. The side of the burner tip burns away some of the wood from the lower feather leaving a "stair-step" from each feather down to the next outer feather. Keep the heat setting on your burner low and make several passes along each line to create the stair-step. If the burner is too hot, it will char the wood making it hard to texture later. This stair stepping can also be done with a small grinding bit (a safe-end diamond cylinder works well) but I find I have more control on the small feathers of a hummingbird if I use a burner.*

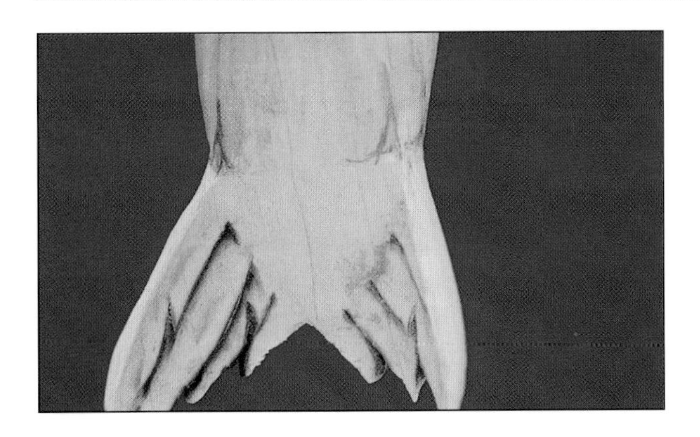

Figure 4:29 *Start working on the underside of the tail by thinning the exposed feather edges (I use a cushioned sanding drum). Redraw the lower tail coverts area and draw the tail feathers on the underside of the bird. Note that on the underside of the tail, only four feathers are showing on each side. Make sure that as the lower tail feather edges go around the tip of the tail, that they line up with the corresponding edges on the upper tail. Repeat the tail covert and feather definition process described above on the bottom of the tail feathers, making sure that the bottom feathers match the top feathers where they go around the tip of the tail.*

Figure 4-30 *Use a similar procedure to add details to each wing. Start on the top of the wing. Draw in the feathers and remove excess wood from around the feather tips. Contour each middle/lesser covert feather. Define each greater covert, secondary, and primary feather with the side of a burner tip. Round over each greater covert, secondary, and primary feather slightly (to give them a subtle convex shape) and undercut a few of them with the knife-edge burner.*

Figure 4:31 *On the underside of the wing, relieve the middle and lesser coverts with your grinder. Thin the overall wing to about 3mm to match the top contour and thin the trailing edge of the wing to a sharp edge. Draw in the wing feathers (including any splits you want to add), making sure the feather edges go around the tip of the wing and meet the corresponding feather edge on the top. Define the feather edges with the side of your burner and round over each feather to give it a slightly convex shape. Even though the primary and secondary feathers have a slightly convex shape on the top surface, the exposed parts of the feathers on the underside of the wing do not generally have a concave shape. As shown in the cross-sectional diagram on the pattern (Figure 4:1), the wing feathers are s-shaped and it is predominantly the convex portion of each feather that you see on both the upper and lower wing surface. This photograph shows both the top and underside of a wing with feathers defined.*

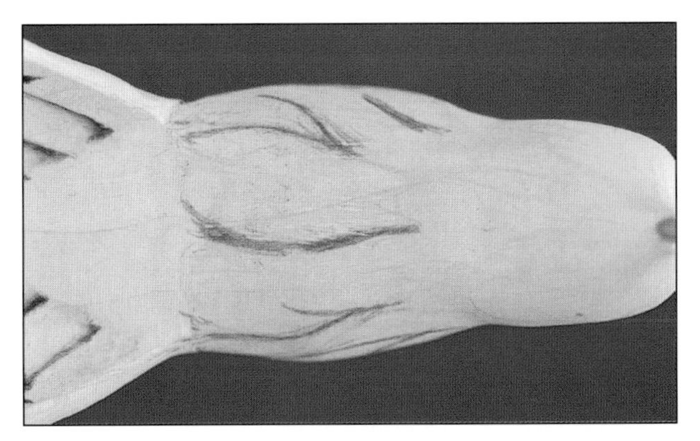

Figure 4:32 *Draw in some gently curved lines on the breast and sides of the bird to outline feather group contours. These feather groups are less noticeable on birds in flight than perched birds and such feather groups generally cannot be seen on pictures of hummingbirds in flight. However, we are going to exercise some artistic license here to add interest to the carving. Remember, though, to keep these contours* subtle. *It will help later if you mark the insertion points for the feet now and draw feather group contours that run through these marks.*

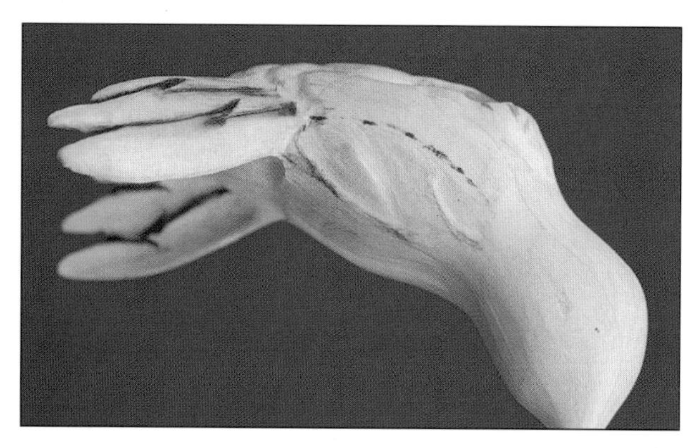

Figure 4:33 *Cut* very shallow *grooves along the contour lines with a small ball or pear-shaped bit and then smooth out the outside edges and round over the inside edge.*

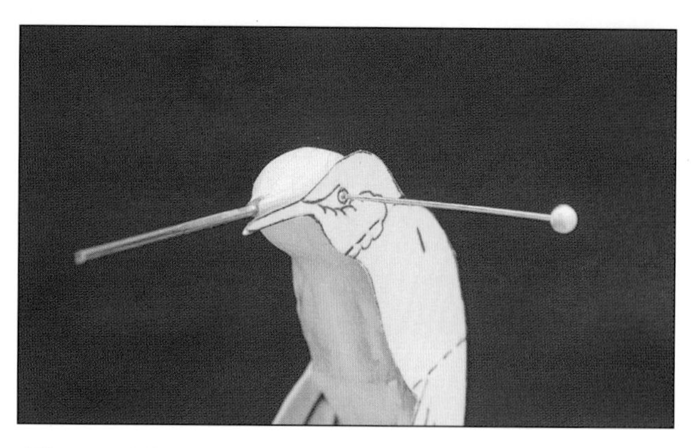

Figure 4:34 *Mark the center of the eye and back edge of the beak on each side of the head. You can either measure these or line-up the side-profile pattern with the side of the head, stick a pin through the center of the eye into the wood to make a mark, then remove the pattern.*

Figure 4:35 *Stick pins in the marks. Look at the pins from the front and top of the head to make sure the eye marks are even. If the eyes are not balanced on both sides, adjust the pins and remark the proper eye location. Also make sure the back of the beak is balanced on both sides.*

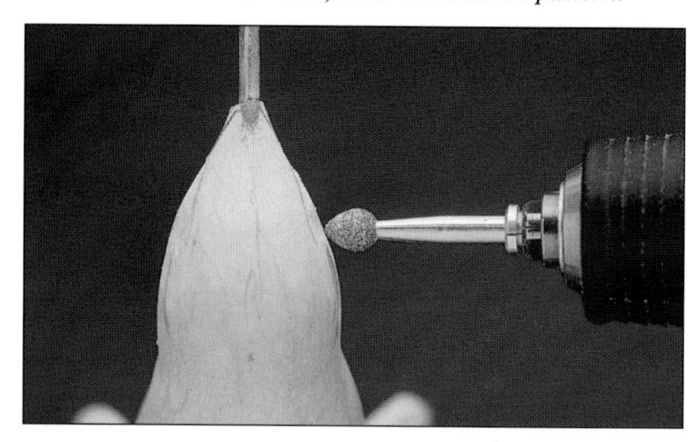

Figure 4:36 *Use any small tapered bit to drill the eye holes to the same diameter as the eyes (3 mm brown eyes will be used for this carving). Make sure that the head width at the front of the eye hole is correct (7mm) and that the top of the eye hole is straight up from the bottom of the eye hole.*

Figure 4:37 *Use a flame-shaped ruby bit or a burning pen to remove the v-shaped area of wood at the back of the beak between the forehead and chin feathers. Then use the flame-shaped bit to create the groove that runs from the front of the eye to the beak. Make sure that this groove has the dip or droop that is characteristic of many hummingbirds. This groove can extend a little behind the eye. Round over the channel into the feathers of the forehead and chin.*

Figure 4:38 *Hollow out the eye sockets with a small ball-shaped bit until the glass eye will fit in the head. Be careful to keep the eye hole opening 3 mm so that you don't have to patch around the eye after it is inserted.*

Figure 4:39 *Draw in the gorget and create* a very shallow groove *along the line with a small ball-shaped bit. Smooth this groove out onto the lower throat, the sides of the neck, and the eye channel, and round the groove over onto the gorget.*

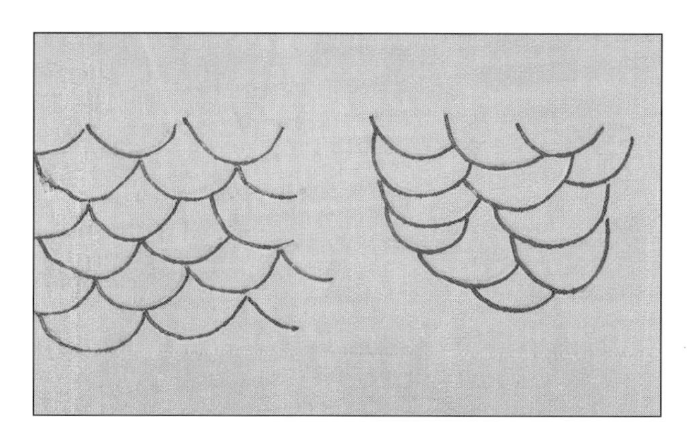

Figure 4:40 *While feathers tend to be in rows, you* do not *want to create perfectly straight rows on your bird. Also, do* not *make the feathers all the same size. If the feathers are all the same size in straight rows (like those on the left), they will tend to look more like scales than feathers.*

Figure 4:41 *Draw individual feathers on the belly, breast, sides, back, and neck of the bird. These feathers are generally smaller toward the head and get larger toward the tail. Also draw individual feathers on the head and gorget (smaller feathers at bill, larger feathers toward neck).*

Figure 4:42 *Next, define each feather (except for the gorget and top of the head) with a small ball-shaped bit (or the side of a tapered stone with a rounded tip) by very subtly cutting around each feather. Then round the groove over onto the feather and smooth it out onto the underlying feather.*

Figure 4:43 *Pre-texture some feathers (body, wing, tail) by running a small ball-shaped bit in the direction of the feather barbs through the feather edges. This pre-texturing adds undulations to each feather, which creates a softer appearance.*

Figure 4:44 *We will use both stoning and burning to create feather barbs in each feather. The burner will be used on the stiff flight feathers and the gorget. Stoning will give a softer look to the fluffier feathers on the rest of the bird. The rule of thumb for texturing is to work from feathers that are underneath to feathers that overlay them (from tail to head, from sides to back and belly).*

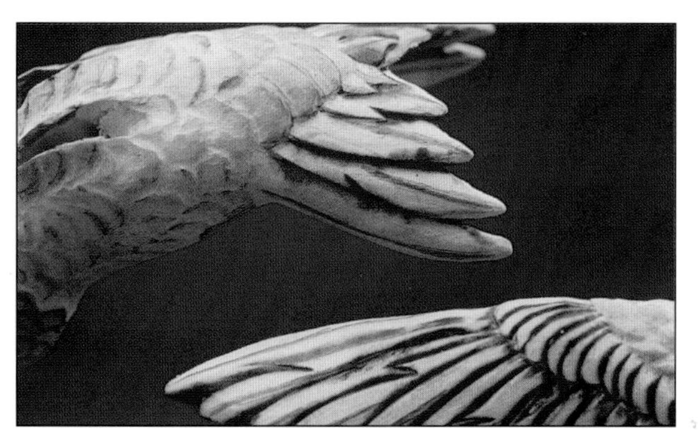

Figure 4:45 *Use a burning pen to texture the stiff feathers in the tail and wings. Start by drawing the quills on the feathers. Each quill should curve slightly and taper to a point towards the tip of the feather. Also, the quills on the center tail feathers, and inside wing feathers, are in the center of the feather; the quills get closer to the leading edge as you go to the outer feathers. You can also define quills on a few of the large tail covert feathers.*

Figure 4:46 *Define the quills by laying your burner tip on its side and drawing it along one side of the quill. Now do the same on the other side of the quill, making sure the raised area between the burn lines tapers to a point near the tip. Remember to keep the burner temperature low so you don't char the wood.*

Figure 4:47 *Before burning feather barbs, draw a few barb lines on each feather to establish the angle the barbs come off the quill and the curve in the barbs. The barbs come off the quill at a fairly sharp angle and curve as they get close to the feather edge. You should burn feathers that lie underneath other feathers first and proceed to the feathers that overlay them. On the top of the tail and wings, this means burning the outer feathers first and working toward the center. On the underside of the tail and wings, you would start with the center, or inside, feathers and work outward.*

Figure 4:48 *Start each burn line at the quill. Draw the burning pen away from the quill (to match the angle of the barb lines you drew on each feather) and curve the burning stroke towards the feather tip. On each feather, burn a few barb lines deeper than the rest, creating minor feather splits; these will be especially noticeable on outside tail and wing feathers. Keep the burn lines as close to each other as possible. Use a fairly low heat setting to avoid charring the wood; burn lines should be light to medium brown.*

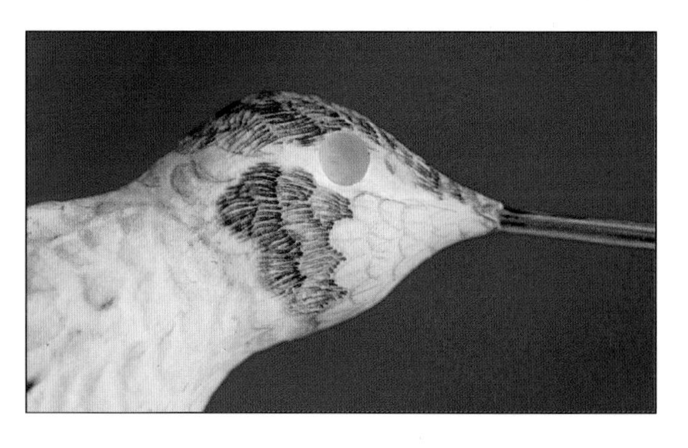

Figure 4:49 *Burning the gorget and top of the head is similar to wings and tail except that we won't define feather quills. Start with the feathers that lie underneath (at the back of the gorget) and work forward. The barb lines should be fanned, curved, and some should extend past the edge of the feather (see Figure 4:50), just as when you are stoning. Dig the pen in a little deeper at the base of each feather (i.e., at the start of each burn stroke) to help define feather edges.*

Figure 4:50 *When stoning body feathers, make sure that the barb lines fan out from the quill in curved lines and that some barb lines extend past the edge of the feather onto the next lower feather. Not doing so will leave you with the unnatural-looking results on the left.*

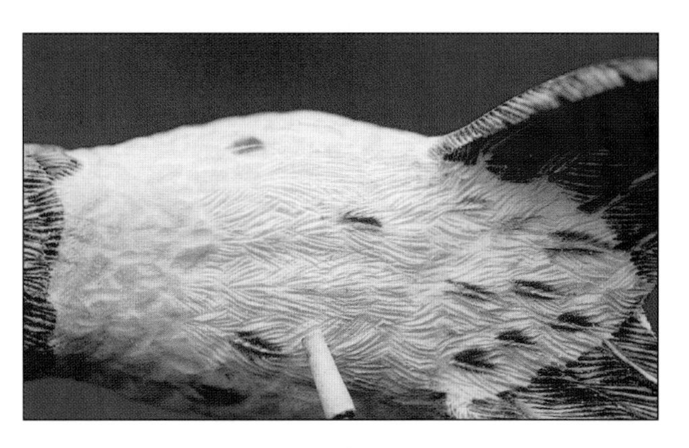

Figure 4:51 *Texture the feathers on the upper and lower tail coverts, the breast and belly, sides and neck, middle/ lesser coverts, and back of the head with a small cylinder or tapered white stone with a flat tip. A work light will create shadows that help you see the texturing you are adding.*

Figure 4:52 *Finally, clean and polish the burning and stoning with a round bristle brush on your grinder. Use a slow speed and a light touch so you don't wear away the texturing.*

Figure 4:53 *To set the eyes, first fill each eye socket with wood putty or filler, cut the wires off the back of the eyes, and push the eyes into the sockets.*

Figure 4:54 *Adjust the eyes in the sockets until they are positioned correctly. I adjust the eyes (in the following order) so they are 1) on the same plane horizontally when viewed from the front (i.e., one eye is not higher or lower than the other).*

Figure 4:55 *2) the same distance back on the head when viewed from the top of the head, 3) pushed into the sockets until they are just visible outside the brow ridge when viewed from the top, 4) straight up and down, and 5) tilted slightly from front to back to follow the wedge shape of the head. I may go through this series of adjustments several times before the eyes look right.*

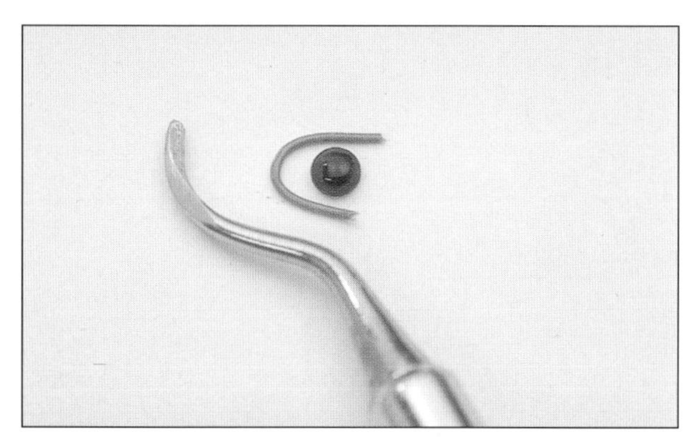

Figure 4:56 *Let the wood putty or filler harden before adding the eye ring; there's nothing more frustrating than finally getting the eyes adjusted correctly, and then pushing one out of adjustment when applying the eye ring. I find it works best to set the eyes the last thing in the evening, and then do the eye rings the next day. To create the eye ring, roll a small amount of two-part ribbon epoxy into a thin string and press it in the gap between the eye and the eye hole using an old dental tool. Cut off any excess.*

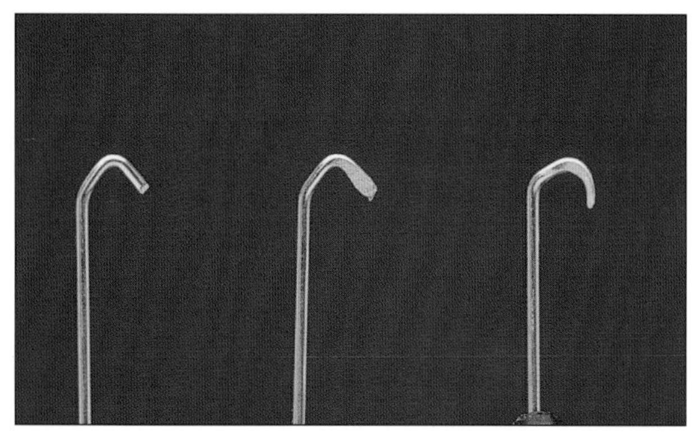

Figure 4:58 *On many photos of hummingbirds in flight, the relatively small feet are not even visible. For this carving, we will expose the last joint and claw of each toe. The foot has four toes, one in back and three in front. The middle toe in front is generally the longest, and the one in back, the shortest. The claws are at a sharp angle to the last joint. The toes are made from 1/16" diameter copper rod. For each toe, cut a 2 cm length of wire (this is much longer than the toe we are making but it gives you something to hold on to while you work). Bend the last 2 mm of each wire with needle nose pliers to form the claw and the next 2 mm to form the last digit of the toe. Place each toe on an anvil and flatten the claw with a hammer. Then shape the claws using a diamond cylinder or flame bit in your grinder.*

Figure 4:57 *Use the dental tool to shape the ribbon epoxy to the correct size and shape. Match the second eye ring to the first. Use a dental tool to blend the outside of the eye ring into the surrounding texturing and to add striations to the eye ring.*

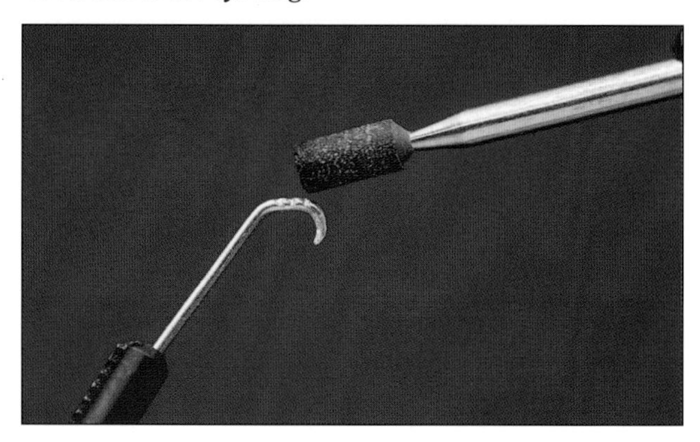

Figure 4:59 *Add scale markings to the toes with a blue cylindrical stone in your grinder or with a hand file, or wait and paint them on later. At the back of the joint (4 mm back from the claw on four toes, slightly shorter for the two back toes, slightly longer for the two middle toes), bend the wire at approximately 45 degrees and cut the wire 4-5 mm past the bend. This last section of each toe will be inserted in the bird.*

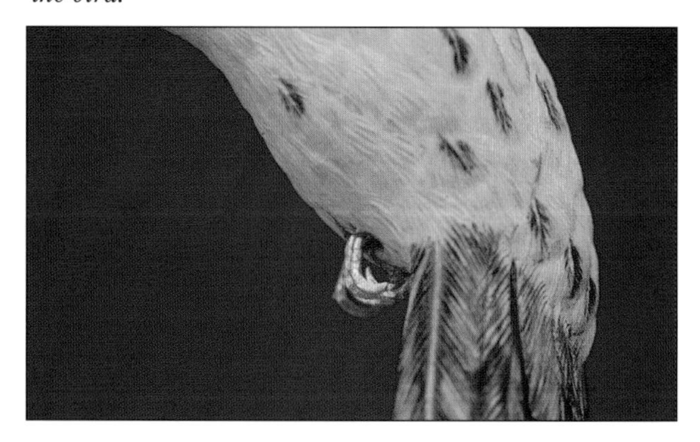

Figure 4:60 *Mark the location for each toe on the belly of the bird and drill 1/16" holes. Apply a drop of 5-minute epoxy to the end of each toe and insert into the holes (make sure you get the correct toes in each hole–shortest ones in back, longest ones in the middle in front).*

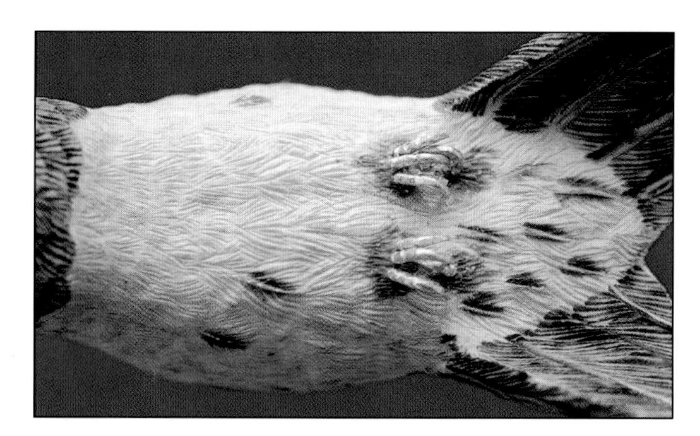

Figure 4:61 *When the glue has dried, use a small amount of two-part ribbon epoxy to fill the holes you drilled. Use a dental tool or* cold *burning tip to texture the epoxy to match the surrounding feathers.*

Figure 4:62 *The final step before painting is to glue the wings in the body with 5-minute epoxy. Put a few drops of epoxy on the end of each wing tab and insert the wings into the body. Do not use too much glue here. If epoxy oozes out of the joint, it will fill in your texturing and will leave a noticeable line where the wing has been glued.´ If there is a gap between the wings and the body after the glue has hardened, fill the gap with ribbon epoxy . Before it sets, texture the ribbon epoxy with a dental tool or a* cold *burning pen just as if you were stoning feathers with your grinder or burning pen. This texturing should blend into the texturing of the adjacent feathers.*

farther towards the feather base to create a softer look. If you want an even softer transition, use a clean brush to gently drag some of the base color back into the edge. This same general technique can be used to accent (lighten or darken) a feather center by dragging the brush from the feather base toward the edge.

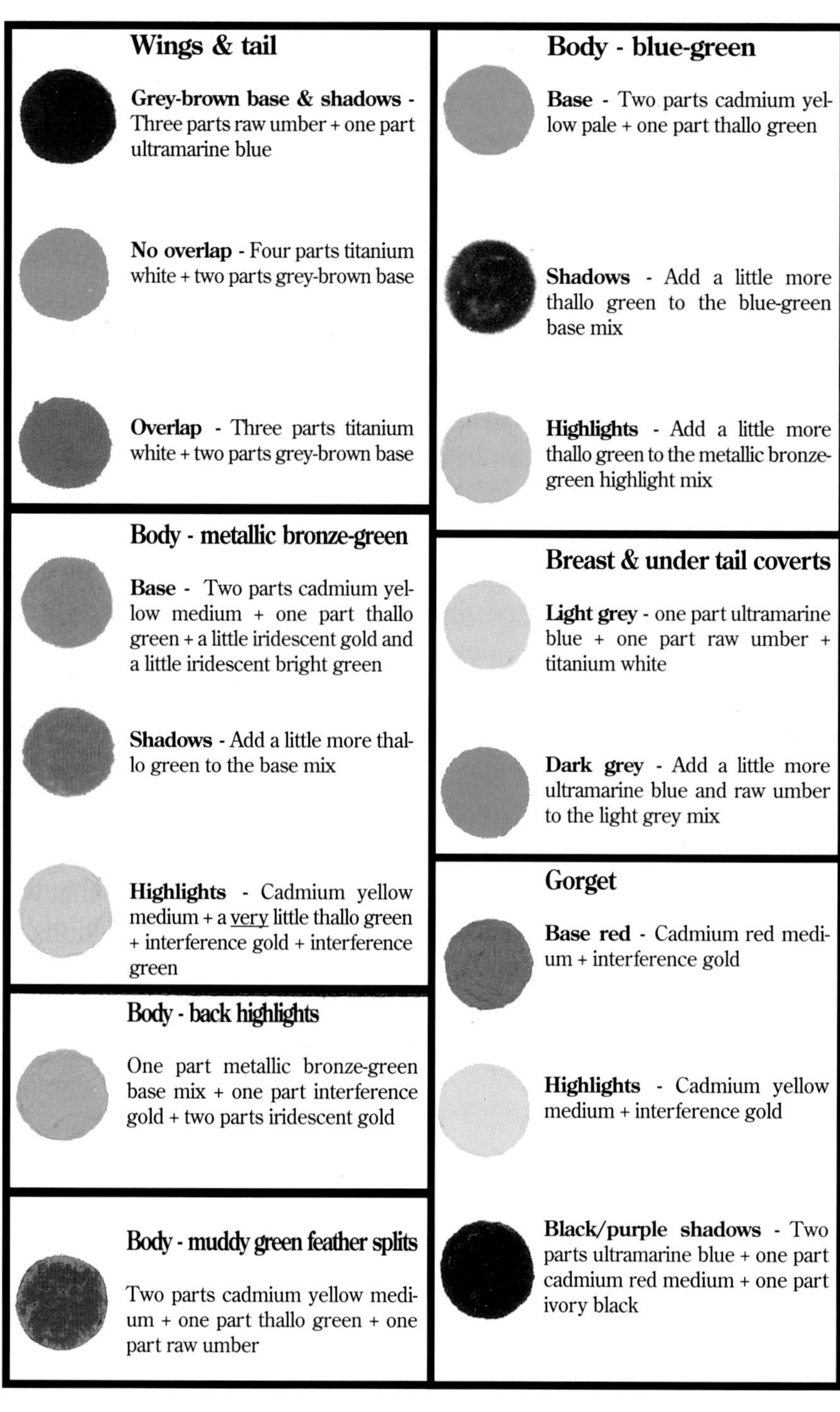

Figure 4:63 *Color mixing guide for ruby-throated hummingbird.*

PAINTING DIRECTIONS

The back of a ruby-throated hummingbird is metallic bronze-green; on males, this green extends down the sides below the wings. Where the light hits the back directly, there are bright yellow-green or yellow highlights; where the light is less direct (e.g., shadows), it is blue-green. The top of the head is also metallic green. The eye channel is black with a small white spot behind the eye. The red gorget has yellow highlights, where the light hits it directly, and black shadows. The breast is grey, with white patches at the throat and the belly. The lower tail coverts generally have darker centers. Wing and tail feathers are a grey-brown; these feathers appear lighter in color when they are spread and the light is coming through them. Directions for mixing these colors are given in Figure 4:63. You should study the photographs of the ruby-throated hummingbird (Figure 1:1) and the similarly colored (except for the gorget) broad-tailed hummingbird (Figures 1:2 and 1:3) in this book, and any other photographs you have of ruby-throated hummingbirds and refer to them throughout the painting process.

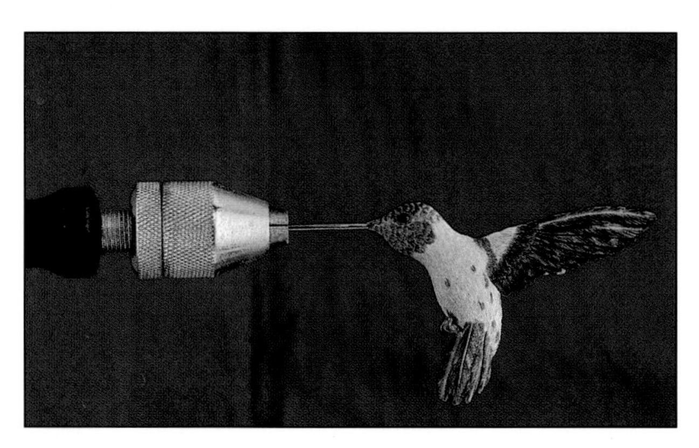

Figure 4:64 *Because of the longer drying times for oil paints, you must be careful when handling the bird as you paint so that you don't smudge previously painted areas. I insert the beak of the bird in a pin vise, which allows me to paint the entire bird without ever touching it with my hands. It doesn't matter if the pin vise messes up the end of the beak, because the beak will be inserted in the flower and won't show.*

Figure 4:65 *Painting starts with the tail (and wings) and moves forward, so that we can paint each feather or feather group overlapping the previously painted feathers or groups. The tail (except the two center feathers) and wings (except the coverts) are grayish-brown. Areas where two feathers overlap are darker, and there is often a subtle shadow where one feather goes underneath an adjacent feather. We will use three shades (values) of the grey-brown color to create these effects.*

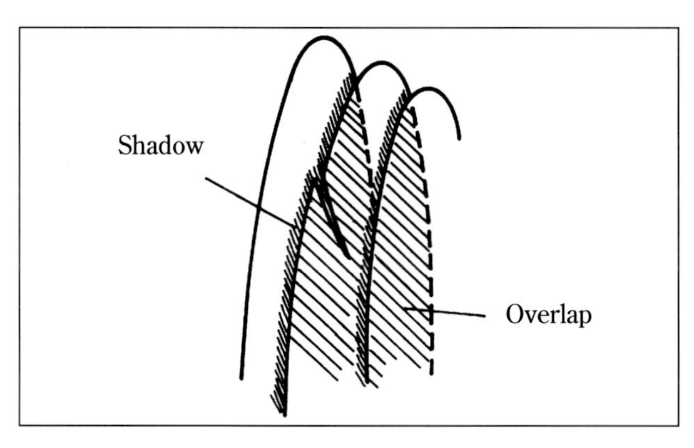

Figure 4:66 *When a hummingbird's wings (and tail) are spread, the light shining through them makes the feathers appear translucent. Where two feathers overlap, the outline of the underlying feather can be seen through the overlapping feather. Areas of overlap are darker than the rest of the feather because the light is being filtered through two layers of feathers where they overlap and only one layer elsewhere. Unfortunately, this effect is not visible on some hummingbird photographs because the powerful, high-speed flash units used to freeze the motion of the bird often overwhelm the natural light filtering through the spread wings. However, recreating this effect on your carving will make the wings appear thinner and more delicate.*

Figure 4:67 *Using a round brush, apply the medium color on each feather where it overlaps the underlying feather (turn the wing or tail over to see where the edge of the underlying feather should be painted on the overlapping feather) and apply the lighter color to areas with no overlap. Then soften the line between the two colors by stippling or wet-on-wet blending (you want to leave a distinct line but with softened edges). In the photo, the outer two wing feathers have been painted; the outer most feather has been blended.*

Figure 4:68 *Use a small liner brush to paint a thin line of the darker color along each feather where it goes under the adjacent feather. This will create a subtle shadow. This color should also be used in the major feather splits you carved, and can be used to paint in additional splits. Stipple or wet-on-wet blend the shadow with the base color.*

Figure 4:69 *Finally, paint the feather quills using the darker color.*

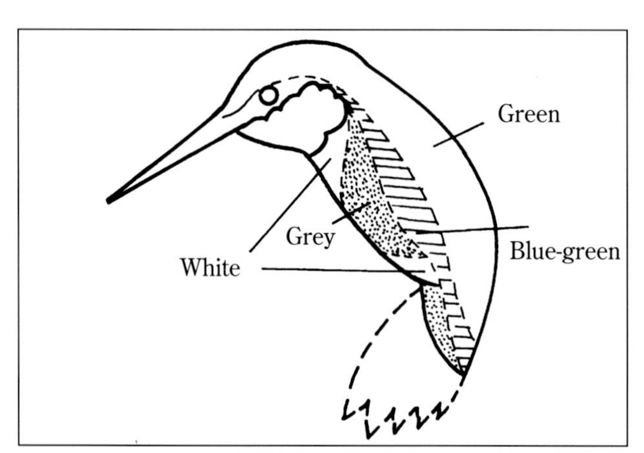

Figure 4:70 *The next step is to add base colors to the body and head. The breast is grey with brighter white at the throat and belly. The tail coverts are also grey. The head and back are green or blue-green depending on the light; on the male ruby-throat, the green/blue-green extends down the sides below the wings. You should refer to Figure 1:1 (a close-up of that figure is shown above) and other photographs of ruby-throated hummingbirds to help determine the location for each base color.*

Figure 4:71 *The appearance of the green body feathers on a ruby-throat depends on how the light hits them. Where the light hits directly, the feathers are bright metallic green with highlights that are almost yellow. Areas that are receding from the light appear more blue-green, while areas out of direct light can appear dull brown. You can see this in Figure 1:3 (of a broad-tailed hummingbird), but remember the dominant source of light is from the flash on the camera so the side of the bird is most directly lit. For this carving, I am assuming that the light is coming from directly overhead. Thus a brighter green will be used as a base color for the top of the back and head and a bluer green for the sides (that are not lit as directly). With the wings in an almost upright position, there are not going to be any deep shadow areas that would appear brown. To determine where the metallic green should grade into the blue-green (and to determine where to paint shadows in later steps), insert the bill of your bird in its base and shine a bright light down on the carving from directly overhead (if you don't have a fairly concentrated beam of light, you may want to move your carving towards the edge of the light in order to better see where highlights and shadows occur).*

Figure 4:72 *Note where the light shines brightest on the back and where the light intensity starts to drop off. This will be a judgment call on your part; on my bird, I painted that transition about halfway between the top of the back and the side.*

Figure 4:73 *Apply the base colors and blend them where they meet using the wet-on-wet blending technique. The goal is to create a soft blend without spreading the blend over a large area. Paint the two center tail feathers and the wing coverts with one of the green colors (depending on whether they are directly lit or in the shadows on your carving).*

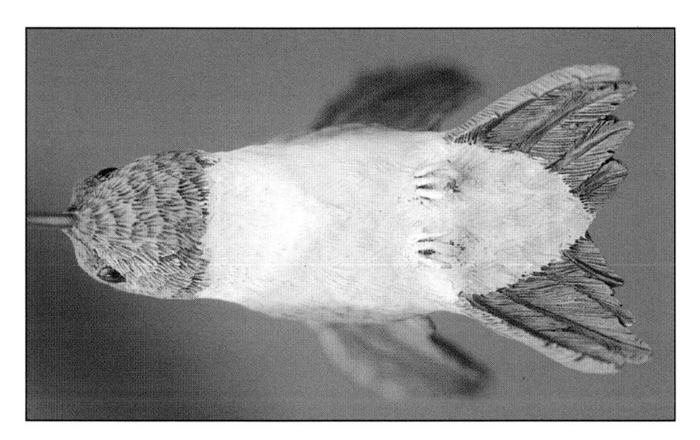

Figure 4:74 *The large under tail coverts have dark centers and lighter edges. Create the darker centers using the technique for accenting feather edges/centers described earlier. Darken the center of each feather with the dark grey mix and use a filbert to soften the dark grey edge.*

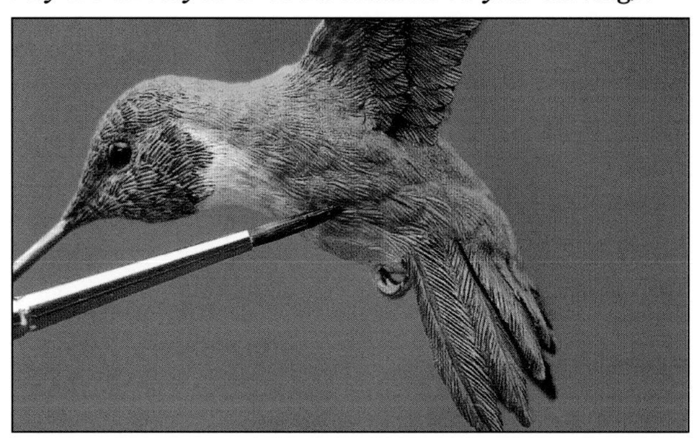

Figure 4:75 *We are now ready to add* shadows *and highlights to the green areas. Place your carving back under the work light so you can see where shadows should be added. Use the metallic bronze-green shadow mix to paint shadows in the metallic green areas and the blue-green shadow color in areas base coated with blue-green. As you add each shadow, stipple or wet-to-wet blend the shadow into the base color. If the base color has soaked into the wood or dried enough to make blending difficult, work on a few feathers at a time by painting each feather (or feather group) with the base color again and then adding the shadow to that feather or feather group. I use a small round brush to apply paint to shadows and a small filbert or blending brush to blend.*

Figure 4:76 *Repeat the procedure to add* highlights *to feathers. I use a small filbert brush (followed by a liner brush) and the technique described earlier for accenting feather edges or centers. The metallic bronze-green highlight mix is used on the top of the back (base coated with metallic green) and the blue-green highlight mix on the sides (base coated with blue-green). Also highlight a few feathers where the blue-green base color blends with the grey breast to further soften this transition.*

Figure 4:77 *Use a similar procedure to add shadows and highlights to the white throat and belly patch and to the grey breast. Use the grey breast color for shadows in white areas. For the breast, use the dark grey mix for shadows and use straight white for highlights. Use the grey breast color to add highlights to a few feathers in the blue-green base color where it blends with the grey breast (a few of these feathers were highlighted with green in the previous step). As with the back, we will add splits and additional highlights later.*

Figure 4:78 *Paint the patch behind the eye white and the rest of the eye channel black, using a 50:50 mix of ultramarine blue and burnt umber. Soften the lines between the eye channel and eye patch, and between the eye channel and the green on the head, by stippling.*

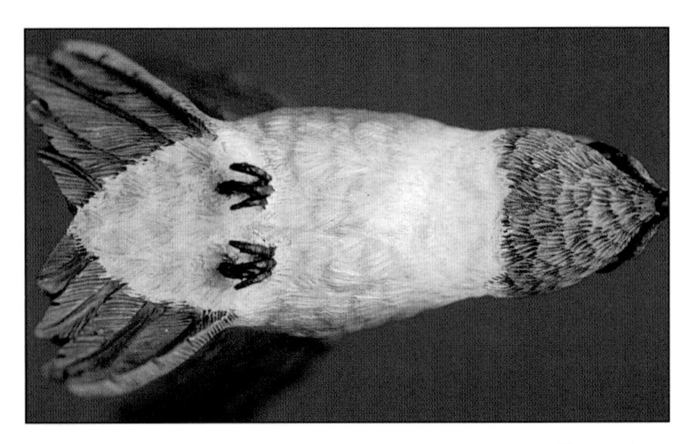

Figure 4:79 *Use the same black to paint the bill and the feet. Lighten the black slightly with titanium white and paint the scales on the toes.*

Figure 4:80 *Base coat the gorget with the cadmium red medium and interference gold paint mix. Place your carving back under the work light and determine which areas of the gorget are most directly lit (yellow highlights) and which areas receive very little light (black shadows). Use the yellow gorget color (and the technique for accenting feather edges) to add highlights. Add shadows (primarily under the chin) with the black-purple mix. Note that some gorget feathers under the chin may be completely black (see Figures 1:1, 1:2, and 1:3).*

Figure 4:81 *We will now add* subtle *shadows to* some *of the feathers on the side of the gorget (see Figure 1:3). Thin the black mix with Liquin, pale drying oil, or other medium that speeds drying time for glazes and improves flow. Load a small round brush with the paint and then remove most of the paint by stroking the brush on your palette or blotting it on a paper towel. Now draw a* thin *line around the back and bottom portions of the feathers you want to shadow. The goal is to darken the area behind and underneath the overlapping feather and have a little of the paint bleed into the texturing of the underlying feather. The consistency of the paint is critical for this step; too thick and it will not bleed into the underlying texture, too thin and it will run all over the gorget. It's hard to describe the proper consistency in words, but a good starting point is the consistency of buttermilk or egg nog.*

Figure 4:82 *Now it's time to make final color adjustments and add details. If the back of your hummingbird does not have enough of the metallic sheen, use the back highlights color mix (with more interference and iridescent gold) to highlight feathers directly in the light. The exact proportions of interference and iridescent gold used in this mix will depend on how much additional metallic sheen you need to add to the back.*

Figure 4:83 *The final painting step is to add little details that soften the appearance and add realism. Feather splits are most effective where one group of feathers overlays a group of differently colored feathers. On a ruby-throated hummingbird, such areas include the green upper tail coverts overlaying the grey-brown tail feathers, the green wing coverts overlaying the grey-brown flight feathers, and the gorget feathers overlaying the throat. Use a fine liner brush to add these splits. Load the brush with the color of the underlying feathers, then create a knife edge on the brush by stroking it on your palette, then turning it over and stroking it on the other side to flatten it out. Use the knife edge of the flattened brush to pull splits from the overlying feathers onto the underlying feathers.*

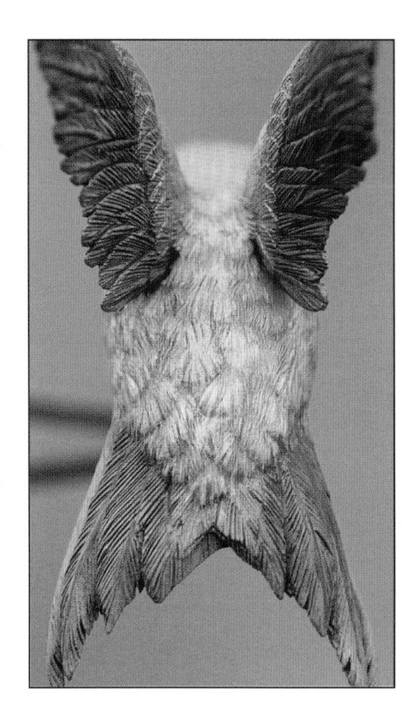

Figure 4:84 *More subtle splits can be added to other parts of the bird by using the flattened liner brush to pull* fine *"lines" of color through the edges of feathers. Use the muddy green mix for splits on the green back and sides. On the breast, use white for splits in the base grey areas, and the base grey for splits in the shadows. The grey can also be used for splits in the white throat and belly. In this photograph, the feathers on the left have had splits added, those on the right have not.*

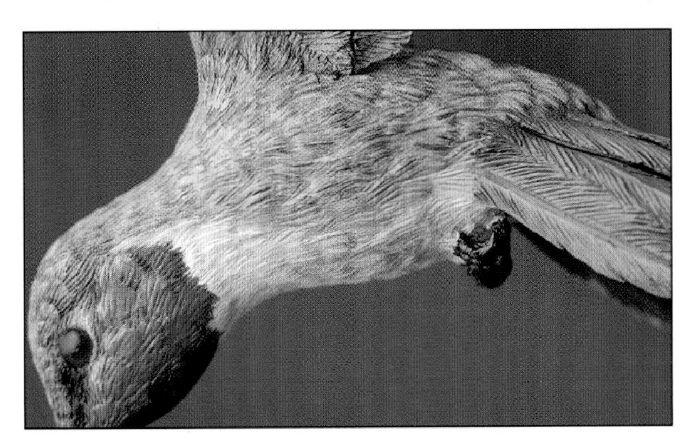

Figure 4:85 *There are some areas on the bird where two colors come together but are not associated with one major feather group overlaying another major group. An example is where the white throat feathers merge into the grey breast feathers and the green side feathers (see Figure 1:3 of a broad-tailed hummingbird). To soften these transitions, use the flattened liner brush to pull fine "lines" of the overlying color into the underneath color. For example, pull fine "lines" of white from the throat into the grey breast and into the green sides. Also pull fine "lines" of grey from the breast into the white belly patch.*

Figure 4:86 *To protect the paint, and to give more of a matte finish, spray the carving with a* matte *Damar varnish. The directions on the can say to let your painting dry for 6 months to a year before applying the varnish. Since the oil paints tend to soak into the wood on carvings, it is generally safe to apply the varnish after a week or so. White oil paints generally take longer to dry than most other oil colors, so you can check the throat and belly areas on your carving to see when they are dry to the touch and when you can apply the varnish. Before spraying varnish, I paint the eyes with black* acrylic *paint (it dries fast and is easy to scrape off) so the varnish doesn't dull them. After the varnish is dry, use a small X-Acto knife to scrape the paint from the eyes.*

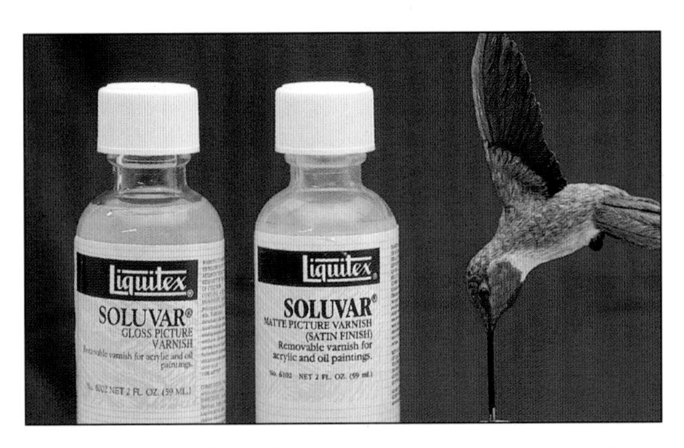

Figure 4:87 *Use a 50:50 mix of matte medium and gloss medium on the bill and feet. Paint the claws with gloss medium.*

Figure 4:88 *The final step is to mount your hummingbird on its base. Apply some 5-minute epoxy to the end of the bill and insert it into the copper tube inside the flower. Check the hummingbird from all sides to make sure it is in the right position (not tilted to one side) and let the glue dry. Finally, glue the stamens into the flower the hummingbird is feeding on (if you didn't do this when constructing the flower).*

Chapter Five

Habitat

Habitat is an integral element of your bird carving. It contributes to the overall design and composition. By providing an environmental context, it helps you tell a story; where the bird is and what it is doing. Finally, it can complement the colors and texture of the bird. However, habitat has limits; too much can overshadow and detract from your carving. Eldridge Arnold, perhaps, summarized it best: "It's easy to overdo this, it's hard to underdo habitat." (Schroeder 1984)

A few guidelines will help ensure that your habitat works well with your bird carving. First, minimize the habitat. A few leaves, flowers, stones, or other habitat components are usually sufficient to provide the environmental context. Second, colors in your habitat should complement the colors of your bird. Painting your habitat with lighter values of the colors used on your bird will look nice and help keep the habitat from overpowering your carving. Another approach is to use complementary colors (opposite on the color wheel) in your habitat to make the bird stand out. Finally, the habitat should be consistent with the bird. For example, if your bird is portrayed in spring breeding plumage, then your habitat should suggest spring time by including something like flower buds. Leaves in fall color might complement the colors of the bird better but would not be consistent with the plumage. Similarly, if you are carving a woodland bird species, your habitat could include branches, leaves, fungi, or other items found in a wooded area. Prairie grasses might look nice, but would be out of character for the bird.

Figure 5:1 *Materials used in constructing the habitat in this chapter include drift wood, a small round base, manzanita root, 3/32" diameter copper tubing, 10-, 12-, 14-, 16- and 24-gauge copper wire, .005" copper sheet, Duro ribbon epoxy, basswood or tupelo, 5-minute epoxy, modeling paste, wood shavings, decorator moss.*

Figure 5:2 *The tools pictured above are used to create habitat for the hummingbird. They include propane and butane torches, a soldering gun, soldering holders, solder and flux, cut-off discs, a sanding sleeve (for Foredom), sandpaper, scissors, high-speed grinder and bits, and a drill and bits.*

REFERENCE MATERIAL

It is important that you have good reference material available when you are making habitat. The best reference is actual plants, branches, leaves, and other habitat components you are trying to reproduce. For example, I have a wide variety of flowers planted in my yard that attract hummingbirds. During the summer, I can go outside and study the plants in detail. At the end of the summer, I collect leaves, flowers, and stems from these plants and put them in a plant press. During the winter, I can use the pressed plants as reference. I also take photographs of the plants during the summer for future use. If you do not have access to actual plants, go to the library and look for plant keys that have good scientific illustrations or photographs. When you go hiking, make a point of collecting (where permissible) interesting driftwood, stones, twigs, seeds, and leaves. It doesn't take long to build your own habitat reference library.

TOOLS AND MATERIALS

Habitat can be made using a wide variety of tools and materials. Various articles and columns in *Wildfowl Carving and Collecting Magazine* and the *Breakthrough Habitat and Exhibit Manual* (Williamson et al. 1987) are good starting points for helpful techniques. For the projects in this book, we will use the tools and materials shown in Figures 5:1 and 5:2.

When making vines or branches from copper tubing and wire, it is extremely helpful to have a good soldering holder ("helping hands"). The small holder in Figure 5:3 from Radio Shack is adequate for small habitat components. The larger holder (from Gesswein) is needed for larger projects. You can also make a small soldering holder using alligator clips, heavy copper wire (e.g., 10 gauge), and a short length of 2x4 (you can also use a firebrick). Cut and strip various lengths of the 10-gauge wire. Crimp an alligator clip on one end of each wire. Drill several holes in the 2x4 the same size as the copper wire. To use your holder, select two or more wires of appropriate length to hold the pieces you are soldering and insert them into

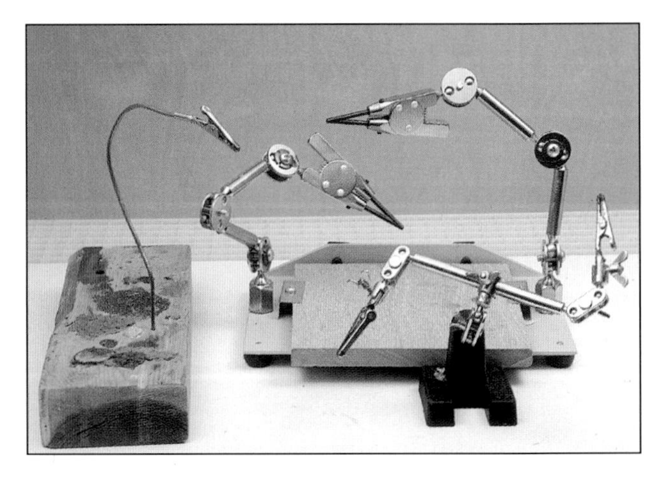

Figure 5:3 A good soldering holder, also known as "helping hands," is a good tool to have when making vines and branches from copper tubing and wire.

holes in the 2x4. Bend the wires as needed and clamp the pieces you are soldering in the alligator clips. It may not be fancy, but it works.

MAKING A DRIFTWOOD BASE

Perhaps the simplest habitat to use with your carving is an interesting piece of driftwood or other weathered wood. Weathered wood can be found almost anywhere; along the shorelines of oceans and lakes, on the banks of rivers, and in wooded areas. Remember, however, that this wood may contain various insects and larvae. To keep these insects from taking up residence in your home, or that of your customers, you should fumigate the wood you collect before using it with your carving. Place the driftwood in a heavy duty plastic bag and spray with a broad spectrum insecticide. It's best to do this outside. Be sure to follow all safety guidelines on the pesticide container and use any recommended protective equipment (e.g., gloves, masks, goggles, respirators)! Seal the plastic bag and let it sit for a week or two. After the driftwood is fumigated, remove it from the bag and let it sit another day or two to allow the smell to dissipate.

Depending on the shape of the driftwood, you may have to cut the bottom on a bandsaw to create a flat spot for mounting to your base. To do the mounting, drill a hole in your base, apply 5-minute epoxy to a piece of copper rod or a short length of coat hanger, and insert the wire in the hole (Figure 5:4). Drill a corresponding hole in the bottom of your driftwood, apply 5-minute epoxy to the wire and driftwood, and insert the wire in the hole. Rubber bands can be used to hold the driftwood in place until the epoxy dries. When the epoxy is dry, add some earth or ground cover (as described next) around the bottom of the driftwood.

Figure 5:4 *To mount the driftwood on the base, drill a hole in the base, apply 5-minute epoxy to a piece of copper rod or a short length of coat hanger, and insert the wire in the hole. A matching hole is drilled in the driftwood and the two are joined together with 5-minute epoxy.*

CREATING EARTH AND GROUNDCOVER

A simple way to create dirt for your habitat is to mix modeling paste with small wood shavings, sawdust, sand, or other materials to achieve the texture you want. I usually add some brown acrylic paint to the mix to get the proper base color. Spread the mix on your base and let it dry. Drybrushing the dried mixture with various paint colors from the rest of your habitat and from your bird will help tie everything together. Another option is to put modeling paste or Kulis Karvit on your base and then press sheet moss (often used in floral arrangements) into the paste or Kulis Karvit before it dries. The base for the broad-tailed hummingbird was finished this way (see page 10).

The base for the hovering hummingbird carving is a red morning-glory mounted in a piece of manzanita root. Red morning-glory vines differ from some of the more familiar garden variety morning-glory vines in several ways. First, the stem is glabrous; this means it is not hairy. Second, flower stems emerge from the crotch formed by the main stem and a leaf stem; these are called axillary peduncles. Third, while the leaves are generally heart-shaped (cordate), they tend to have lobes at the base. Fourth, the flower is more tube-like (i.e., the sides are almost parallel) for most of its length and flares out primarily at the tip. Many other morning-glory vines taper more evenly from the base to the tip. Finally, the stamens (the pollen-bearing parts of the flower) extend past the end of the flower (they are exserted). Keeping these features in mind when building the vine will help you to accurately duplicate this plant species. A pattern for the flower parts is provided in Figure 5:5.

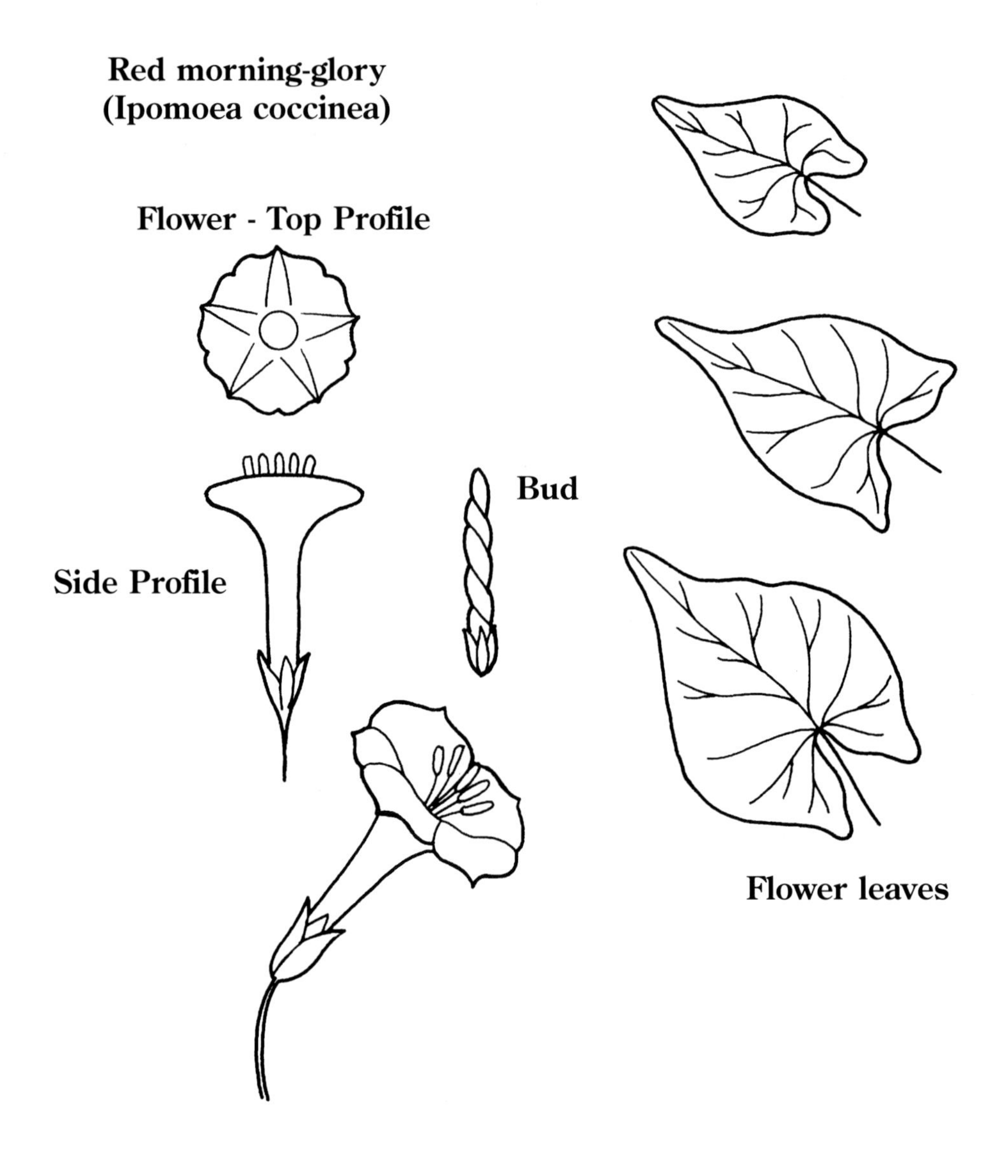

Figure 5:5 *Pattern for red morning-glory parts.*

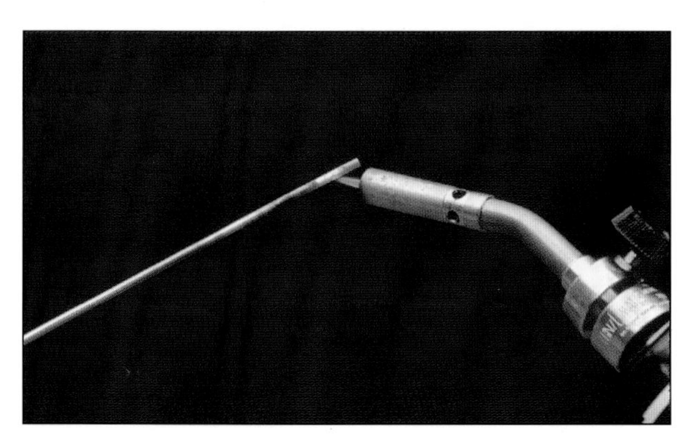

Figure 5:6 *The lower portion of each main stem is made from 1/8" copper tubing. Heat the tubing to red hot with a propane torch; this will detemper the tubing and make it easier to bend.*

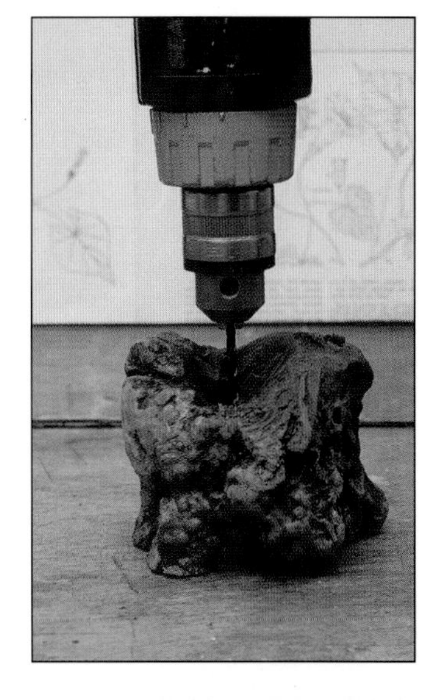

Figure 5:7 *Drill three 3/16" holes near the center of the manzanita root. Insert copper tubing in two of the holes and start twining them together (like morning-glory vines twine together). As you are twining the tubing, create a nice soft curve that starts to one side and then goes upward (see Figure 5:10).*

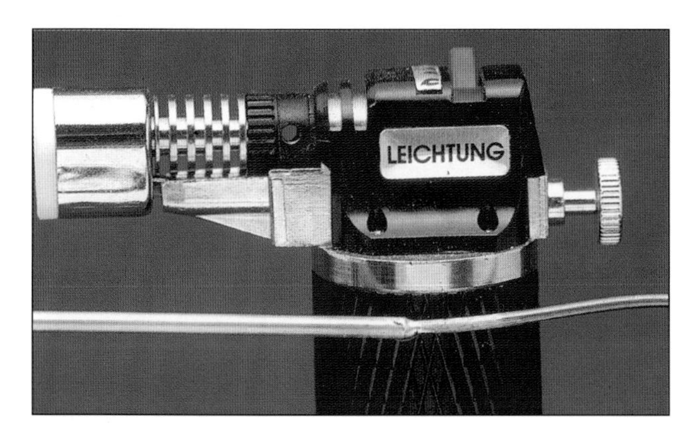

Figure 5:8 *The upper portion of each main stem is made from 12 gauge copper wire. Strip the wire, then sand and flux the end that will be inserted in the copper tubing. Insert the fluxed wire at least 1" into the tubing so that when you taper the tubing to hide the connection there is enough of the solder joint left to make a strong connection. Clamp the wire and tube in your soldering holder to keep them from moving while you solder. Heat the connection with a propane or butane torch (I find the small butane torches much easier to use for these connections). When the connection is hot enough (the flux should bubble and then turn clear), touch the solder to the joint and the solder should flow down into the tube. If the solder melts but won't flow into the joint, then either the surfaces are not clean enough (sand them again) or there isn't enough flux (pull the pieces apart and apply more flux).*

Figure 5:9 *When the joint has cooled, use a sanding sleeve or disk to taper the tube and smooth it into the wire to hide the joint.*

Figure 5:10 *When the top portion of each stem has been soldered to its tube, continue twining the wires together until you get the desired length and shape. Cut off any excess wire. Using your sketch as a reference, mark on each main stem the locations where the leaf and flower stems will attach. Note that the stems have been temporarily attached in this photograph so you can see where I put mine.*

Figure 5:11 *The lower leaf and flower stems (the ones that will be attached to the copper tube) are made from 14 gauge copper wire. For each leaf/flower stem pair (there are two such pairs on this vine), flatten one end of each wire and solder together.*

Figure 5:12 *Using a cutoff wheel, cut a notch out of the main stems where each leaf/flower stem pair will attach.*

Figure 5:13 *Taper the soldered end of the leaf/flower stems with a sanding sleeve so that the end will fit down into the notch.*

Figure 5:14 *Flux the soldered end of a leaf/flower stem pair, insert it into the notch and clamp with your soldering holder. Solder using a small butane torch. Smooth the solder joint and soldered wires into the main stem with a sanding sleeve. If solder does not completely fill the notch, fill it with modeling paste and sand smooth when it dries.*

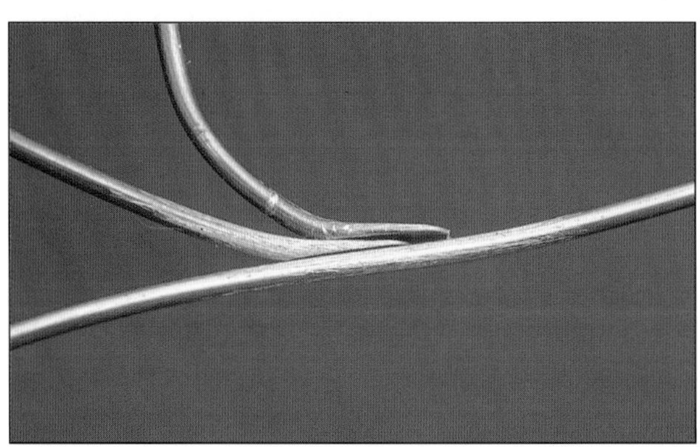

Figure 5:15 *The upper leaf/flower stems (the ones that will attach to the copper wire) are made from 16 gauge wire and will be soldered to the main stems with butt joints. Flatten each leaf and flower stem where it will attach to the main stem. Sand and flux the flattened portions and clamp in place with your soldering holder. Solder with a butane torch. When cool, smooth the joint with a sanding sleeve.*

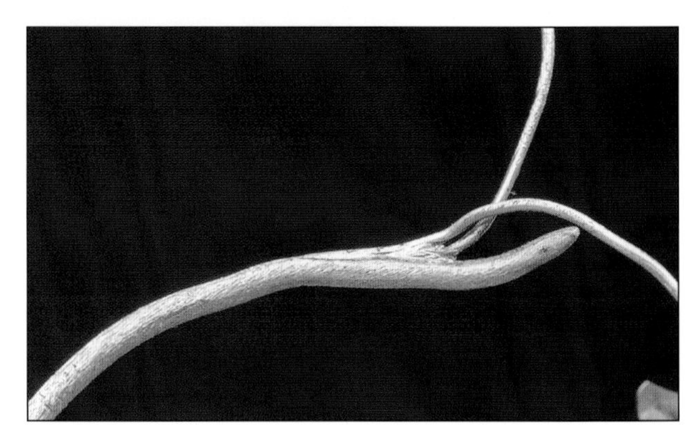

Figure 5:16 *The short main stem coming out of the manzanita root is made from 10 gauge copper wire with 16 gauge flower and leaf stems attached with a butt joint.*

Figure 5:17 *The five steps in making a leaf are shown in the photograph from left to right. First, trace around the pattern for each leaf (1 large, 1 medium, 3 small) on .005" thick copper sheet and cut out with scissors. Second, draw the veins on each leaf; make a very subtle s-shaped curve for the main vein and curve each of the side veins somewhat. Third, place a leaf on a carving catalog (or other surface with some give to it) and press in the veins with a dental tool. The veins are on the bottom of the leaf; press from the top leaf surface so the veins stick out on the bottom. Fourth, flip the leaf over on the carving catalog and rub the bottom surface between the veins in a circular motion with a rounded dowel. This will raise the upper leaf surface from the veins and will give some fullness to the leaf. Finally, gently bend the edges of each leaf to create an uneven waviness in the edges.*

Figure 5:18 *The two leaves at the top of the vine are just forming, as are the associated flower buds. Roll the edges of these leaves over so that it looks like they are just uncurling. It may help to roll these edges over a small diameter dowel so that they roll rather than bend.*

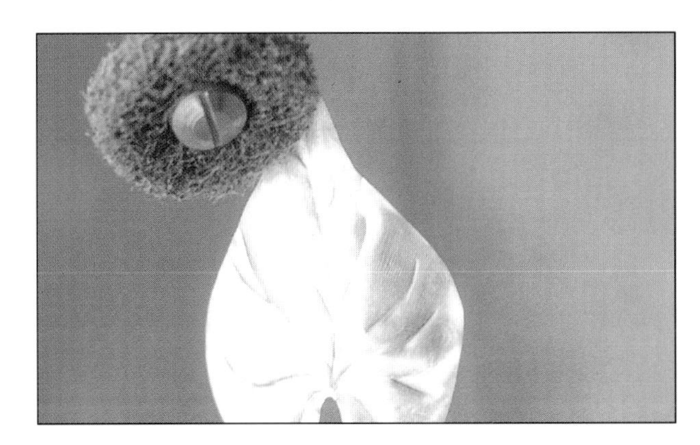

Figure 5:19 *Use a Scotch-Brite pad in your grinder to soften the surface of each leaf.*

Figure 5:20 *Taper the end of each leaf stem (remember that the leaf stems are the ones on the outside of each pair, the flower stems are between the leaf stem and the main stem) with a sanding sleeve. Clamp the leaf and the vine in your soldering holder and adjust so that the tapered leaf stem runs along the center vein of the leaf. Flux the stem and solder to the leaf with a soldering gun. Repeat until all leaves are attached.*

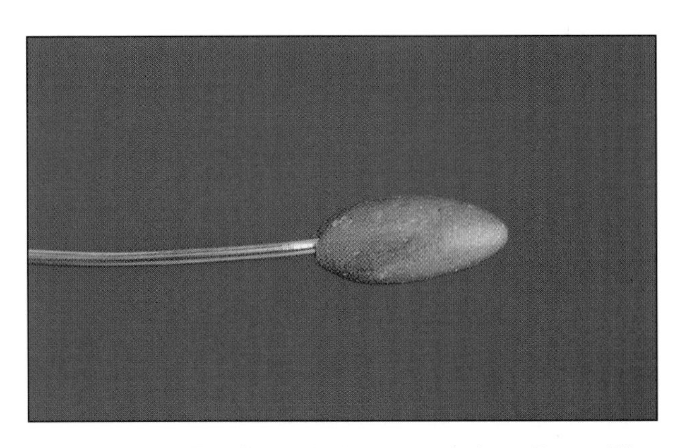

Figure 5:21 *The flower buds are made from Duro ribbon epoxy. Cut a small length of ribbon epoxy, cut out the thin, hard area where the blue and yellow meet, then knead the two colors together until the epoxy turns green Push a small ball of epoxy on the end of each stem and shape into a bud.*

Figure 5:22 *Trace the patterns for the flowers and the large flower bud onto 1" thick tupelo or basswood and cut out with a bandsaw or coping saw.*

Figure 5:23 *For the large flower bud, round the base and taper and round over the tip. Draw five spiralling lines from the base to the tip and create grooves along the lines with a small ball-shaped bit or a writing tip in a wood burner. Sand smooth with 400 grit sandpaper.*

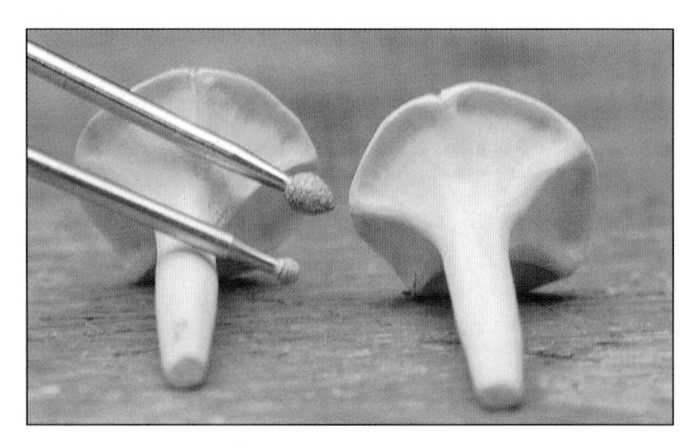

Figure 5:24 *Using a pear-shaped bit, shape the outside of each flower. Mark the five points of the flower petals and define the points by creating a scalloped edge on the flower.*

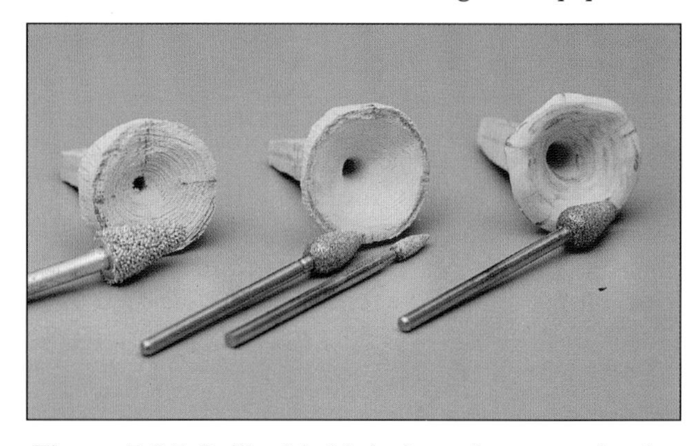

Figure 5:25 *Drill a 3/32" hole down the center of each flower from the top (the large end). Using a small carbide kutzall, then large and small flame-shaped bits, and finally a pear-shaped bit, hollow out the inside of the flower until it matches the outside shape.*

Figure 5:26 *Be careful that you don't grind through the wood when shaping the inside! Two tricks will help prevent this. First, hold the flower so that one of your fingers is outside the flower at the place you are grinding. If your finger starts to get warm, the wood is getting thin. Second, periodically hold the flower between you and a bright light. Places where you can see light through the wood are very thin.*

Figure 5:27 *From each point of the flower petals, draw diverging lines about halfway down into the flower. Very lightly burn along each line with a writing tip on a wood burner to define the "stripes" inside the flower. Finally, sand the flowers smooth with 400-grit sandpaper.*

Figure 5:28 *Cut a short (3/4") piece of 3/32" diameter copper tube and solder it to the end of the flower stem that will support the hummingbird. The flower stem should extend about halfway into the tube, leaving the other half open to insert the beak of the hummingbird.*

Figure 5:29 *For the flower that will support the hummingbird, drill a 7/64" hole in the base, apply 5-minute epoxy to the outside of the tube, and push the flower onto the tube until the tube is covered (don't get epoxy in the tube). For the other flower, drill a 5/64" hole in the base and glue to the flower stem with 5-minute epoxy. Drill a 1/16" hole in the flower bud and glue to its stem.*

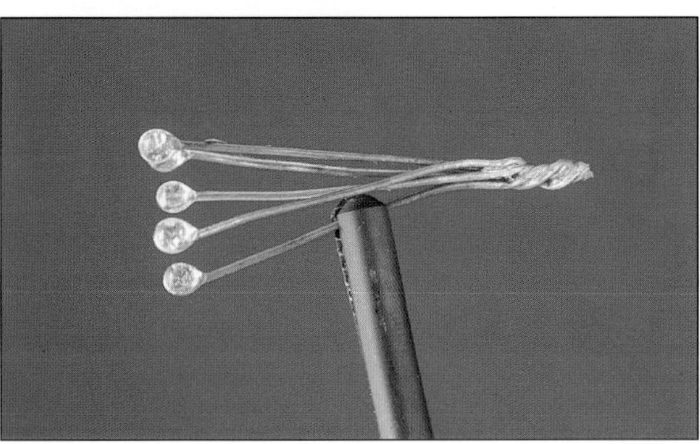

Figure 5:30 *To make each set of stamens, cut 5 strands of 24 gauge copper wire, twist the bases together, and solder. Insert the soldered end into one of the flowers and cut all the wires so that they extend past the end of the flower by about 1/8". Using 5-minute epoxy or a hot glue gun, put a drop of glue on the end of each wire.*

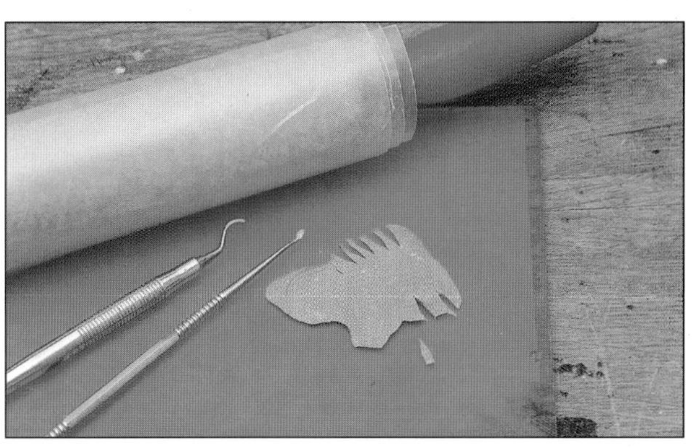

Figure 5:31 *The sepals (the small "leaves" at the base of each flower and bud) are made from Duro ribbon epoxy. Knead a small ball of epoxy until it is green, put it between two pieces of wax paper, and roll thin with a rolling pin. Cut individual sepals (there are 5 per flower) with an X-Acto knife.*

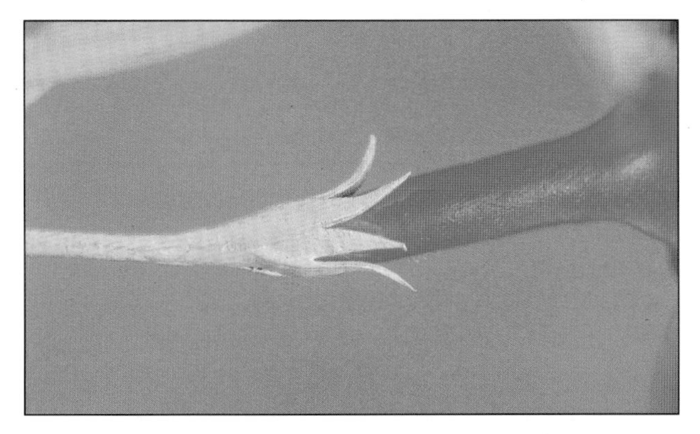

Figure 5:32 *Pinch and taper the edges of each sepal and press them onto the base of a flower. When all 5 are on, pinch off any excess at the base and blend the epoxy into the stem. For variety, the tips of some sepals should be against the flower, while others are curled away from the flower.*

Figure 5:33 *Use a Q-Tip and rubbing alcohol to remove any remaining flux from the solder joints. Then use a course (brown) Scotch-Brite pad mounted on a mandrel in your high speed grinder to roughen up all metal surfaces. Finally, spray the vines (and flowers and buds if painting with acrylics) with Testor's Dull Cote to seal the metal. If not sealed, the metal can oxidize over time and discolor your paint.*

Figure 5:34 *Use 5-minute epoxy to glue the vines into the holes in the manzanita root. Use a mix of modeling paste, wood shavings, and raw umber acrylic paint as discussed earlier to create a little bit of dirt around the base of the stem.*

Figure 5:35 *The morning-glory can be painted with either acrylic or oil paints (see "Paints and Brushes" page 9 and "Supplies and Techniques" page 42), using brushes, an airbrush or both. Since the hovering hummingbird for this base will be painted with oil paints, we will use oil paints for the flower.*

Figure 5:36 *The paint mixes used on the base are generally lighter values of colors used to paint the bird (see the color mixing guide for the ruby-throated hummingbird–Figure 4:63). For the leaves and stem, we will use the base green (metallic bronze-green) color of the hummingbird (without the interference and iridescent paints) and two slightly lighter shades of this green. Mix all of these colors now because we will blend them together while they are wet. Three values of green will be used on each leaf.*

Figure 5:37 *Paint the leaves and stem with the medium green color. Then, using a liner brush or an airbrush and the dark green, paint the veins that are pressed in the leaf. If you are painting with brushes instead of an airbrush, stipple the veins lightly while the two colors are still wet to soften the line between the veins and the leaf. Oil paints are really helpful here because their long drying time gives you plenty of time to stipple.*

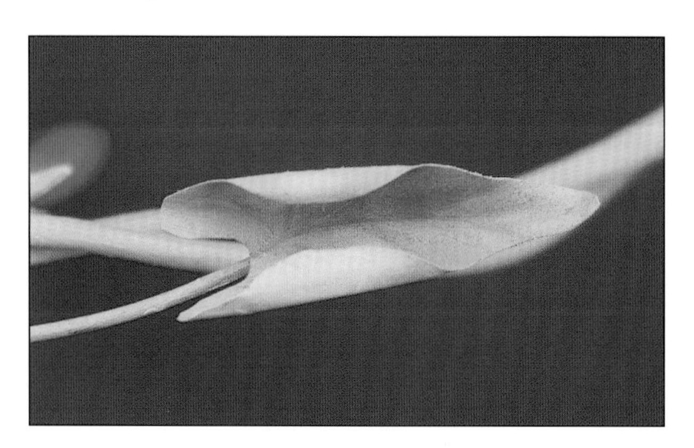

Figure 5:38 *Using the light green, add some lighter highlights to the leaf and lighten some of the edges. To determine where the highlights should be added, shine a bright light from directly overhead (we will assume the light source is directly overhead as we paint both the morning-glory and the hummingbird) and notice where the light strikes the leaf most directly. I prefer using an airbrush because it produces more subtle highlights and blends that have a softer look. As an alternative, you can add these highlights with a brush while the base color is still wet and stipple to blend.*

Figure 5:39 *Dry brush several of the greens used for the leaves, on the dirt you created around the base of the stems. You can also dry brush some of the lighter and darker greens on the stem.*

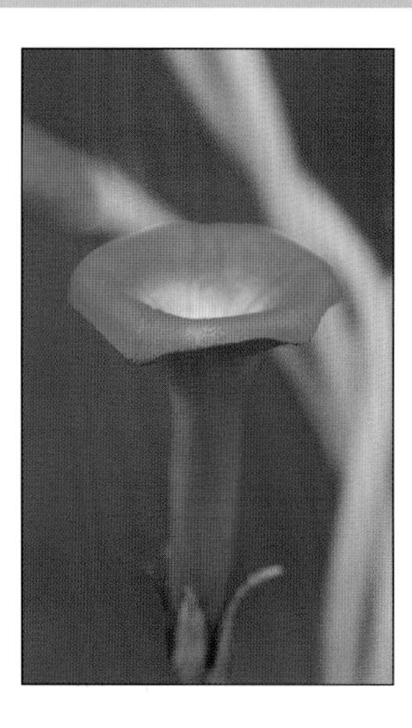

Figure 5:40 *The flowers are painted with cadmium red medium lightened with a little titanium white and cadmium yellow medium. Add highlights and shadows with an airbrush (or use a brush and stipple to blend). Highlights are added with cadmium yellow medium on the petal edges, in the center of the flower, and on the ribs on the outside. Use the red color darkened with a little dark green (the complementary color of red) to add shadows under the lip of the petals. The large flower bud is painted similarly; start with the base red color, add shadows in the grooves, and very subtly lighten the tip of the bud with yellow. The two smaller buds are painted with the red base*

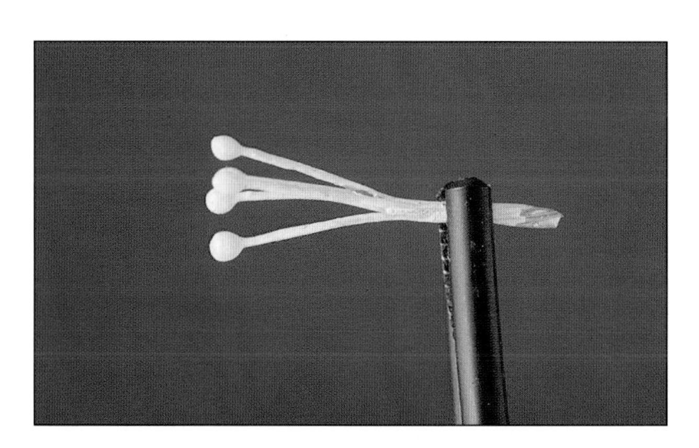

Figure 5:41 *Paint each set of stamens with yellow-white stems (titanium white with a little cadmium yellow medium) and yellow heads. When dry, use 5-minute epoxy to glue into each flower. Make sure you don't get any epoxy in the tube for the hummingbird beak. It helps to insert a scrap piece of 1/16" rod in the tube while you are gluing the stamens. Remove the rod before the epoxy dries, however, so it doesn't accidentally get glued in. If you prefer, you can glue the stamens after painting and mounting your hummingbird.*

Figure 5:42 *If you painted the morning-glory with oil paints, let it dry to the touch (about a week or so) and then spray with a* matte *finish Damar varnish. Cover the manzanita root with newspaper or Saran Wrap before spraying so that the varnish does not get on the wood.*

References

Biel, T. L. 1985. *Zoobooks 2: Hummingbirds.* Wildlife Education, Ltd. San Diego, CA. np.

Browning, N. L., and R. Ogg. 1988. *The Mystery and Miracle of Hummingbirds.* Terrell Publishing Inc., Kansas City, MO. 32 pp.

Burk, B. 1988. *Game Bird Carving.* Winchester Press, New Century Publishers, Piscataway, NJ. 383 pp.

Greenwalt, C. H. 1960. *Hummingbirds.* Garden City, NY. Doubleday and Co. Reprinted in 1990 by Dover Publications, Inc., New York. 162 pp.

Johnsgard, P. A. 1983. *The Hummingbirds of North America.* Smithsonian Institution Press, Washington, D.C. 303 pp.

Narosky, T. and D. Yzurieta. 1987. *Guia para la Identificacion de las Aves de Argentina y Urugay.* Asoc. Ornitologica del Plata, B. Aires. 345 pp.

Noll, J. 1995. "Beginner's Notebook: Color Notes." *Wildfowl Carving and Collecting.* Spring 1995: 66-68.

Schroeder, R. 1984. *How to Carve Wildfowl.* Stackpole Books, Harrisburg, PA. 225 pp.

Skutch, A. F., and A. B. Singer. 1973. *The Life of the Hummingbird.* Crown Publishers, Inc., New York. 95 pp.

Stokes, D., and L. Stokes. 1989. *The Hummingbird Book.* Little, Brown and Company, Boston, MA. 89 pp.

Toops, C. 1992. *Hummingbirds: Jewels in Flight.* Voyageur Press, Inc., Stillwater, MN. 128 pp.

Tyrell, E. Q., and R. A. Tyrrell. 1984. *Hummingbirds: Their Life and Behavior.* Crown Publishers, Inc., New York. 212 pp.

Weidensaul, S. 1989. *Hummingbirds.* Portland House, New York. 144 pp.

Wilcox, M. 1989. *Blue and Yellow Don't Make Green.* North Light Books, Cincinnati, OH.

Williamson, B., K. Edwards, J. Hall, and D. Blair. 1987. *The Breakthrough Habitat and Exhibit Manual.* Breakthrough Publications, Loganville, GA. 156 pp.